Hmayeak Shēms
A Poet of Pure Spirit

Vahé Baladouni and John Gery

UNIVERSITY PRESS OF AMERICA,® INC.
Lanham • Boulder • New York • Toronto • Plymouth, UK

Copyright © 2010 by
University Press of America,® Inc.
4501 Forbes Boulevard
Suite 200
Lanham, Maryland 20706
UPA Acquisitions Department (301) 459-3366

Estover Road
Plymouth PL6 7PY
United Kingdom

All rights reserved
Printed in the United States of America
British Library Cataloging in Publication Information Available

Library of Congress Control Number: 2009942758
ISBN: 978-0-7618-5054-0 (paperback : alk. paper)
eISBN: 978-0-7618-5055-7

Cover image: Hmayeak Shēms by Ashot Zorian

∞ ™ The paper used in this publication meets the minimum requirements of American National Standard for Information Sciences—Permanence of Paper for Printed Library Materials, ANSI Z39.48-1992

This publication is made possible by a generous grant from The Dolores Zohrab Liebmann Fund.

Contents

List of Photographs	vii
Preface	ix
Acknowledgments	xiii
Reference Key	xv
A Chronology of Hmayeak Shēms	xvii
A Diasporan Journey: Cities Where Shēms Visited and Lived	xix

Part I: Student, Rebel, and Wandering Dervish: From Trabzon to the Caucasus and the Balkans — 1

Prologue: Shēms, the Dervish—"that Hapless, Tattered Nobleman"	1
Growing Up in Trabzon	4
A Turbulent Secondary School Education	7
Heading for Ējmiatsin and Erevan	12
First Teaching Appointment	14
The Day the Sun Darkened: the Armenian Genocide of 1915	15
The Aftershock	17
A Reunion of Survivors	21
A Voice from the Depths of the Soul	22

Part II: Poet, Scholar, Orator, and Teacher: Alexandria 29
Making Sense of His New Environment 29
Flight to Paris 36
Moment of Truth 37
Two Publications: *Ṛoshnakan* and *Sayat' Nova* 43
Chashka Chaï: Around a Cup of Tea 45
Repatriation: *Depi erkir* [Homeward Bound!] 48
Serving the Word and Poetry 49
The Passion that Chose Shēms 57
His Waning Years 60
Epilogue: Hmayeak Shēms—this Man, this Poet 64

Appendix A: "A Portrait of Hmayeak Shēms" by Gurgēn Mkhit'arian 69
Appendix B: "The Hmayeak Shēms I Knew" by Step'an Shahpaz 75
Appendix C: An Undated Draft Letter to Levon Hovhannēsian Written by Hmayeak Shēms 79
Notes 83
Acronyms and Abbreviations 93
Selected Bibliography 95
Index 99

Photographs

Photo 1.1.	An Ascetic Shēms, Trabzon, Turkey, c. 1921	20
Photo 2.1.	A Meditative Shēms, Alexandria, Egypt, 1924	31
Photo 2.2.	Faculty of Poghosian National School, Alexandria, Egypt, 1925	33
Photo 2.3.	Family Reunion, Zagazig, Egypt, 1928	39
Photo 2.4.	Gurgēn Mkhit'arian with Shēms, Alexandria, Egypt, early 1940s	50

Preface

Since the publication of a selection of Hmayeak Shēms's prose poems under the title of *For the House of Torkom* in 1999, John Gery and I had, on and off, talked about presenting this Armenian diasporan poet to the English reading public more widely. Of the various possible approaches to the task—as a Shēms reader, documentary biography, literary review, critical biography—we finally settled on the last one. As a critical biography, *Hmayeak Shēms: A Poet of Pure Spirit* aims at re-creating Shēms's life by combining his personal history with his works. Thus we have freely invoked lines from Shēms's poems as well as his prose writings to illuminate his life, while drawing on the events of his life to shed light on his works. By so doing, we believe a more genuine, revealing, and complete image of Shēms has emerged. We also believe that we have been able to achieve this without undue intrusion of criticism upon the continuity of the poet's life or generating unwarranted interpretations of the works that may distort the character of the subject.

In my capacity as Hmayeak Shēms's long-time biographer, his literary executor, and a student of his works, I feel I am well suited to undertake such a biography. As a member of Shēms's extended family, I lived and broke bread with him for over twenty years under the same leaking roof. Also, from a very young age I started attending Shēms's lectures and public speeches. Finally, on occasion, I was privileged to be part of a group of his disciples who met with him on a weekly basis to discuss literary, educational, and national affairs. In short, I have witnessed the many facets of Shēms's public and private life from the 1930s until his untimely death in 1952. In the years since his death, I have maintained a rich correspondence with many who have known him, his work, or both. I have also researched the sources of his ideas and the background of the various parts of the world he traveled. On his part, John Gery, poet, critic, and professor of modern poetry and creative writing, brings to this endeavor his own poetic sensibilities and literary insights as well as having collaborated with me on translating Shēms's works. While neither a speaker nor a reader of the Armenian language, John has helped to shape this biography by bringing to bear his critical eye on Shēms's life and works.

John and I had barely made a start on this biography when on 29 August 2005 Hurricane Katrina devastated New Orleans and ravaged my home at 18 Chatham Drive, New Orleans, LA 70122 where Shēms's archive—manuscripts, personal papers, photographs, and paraphernalia—was stored. During this catastrophic event, Shēms's archive, which had been in my safekeeping for well over half a century, along with my extensive personal library, suffered considerable loss. The salvaged materials were later transported to Falls Church, Virginia, where my family was evacuated. Here, over several months, during which period I also underwent heart surgery, they were painstakingly dried, dehumidified, cleaned of their mold, and restored to near usable condition. Despite this odyssey, work on the biography continued, though admittedly at a snail's pace. Now that the biography has come to a conclusion, the remnants of Shēms's surviving archive, including the unpublished letters and memoirs, will be transferred to the Eghishē Ch'arents'[1] Museum of Literature and Art in Erevan, Armenia, for inclusion in Shēms's permanent archive there.

TRANSLATION

It is said that the translation of any work of literature is wrought with many difficulties, but none more so than poetry. "Poesy is of so subtle a spirit," writes Sir John Denham (1615-1669) in his Preface to *The Destruction of Troy* (1636), "that in pouring out of one language into another, it will all evaporate." In a similar vein, over a century and a half later, Percy Bysshe Shelley (1792-1822), in his "A Defense of Poetry," would write: ". . . the vanity of translation; it were as wise to cast a violet into a crucible that you might discover the formal principles of its color and odor, as to seek to translate from one language into another the creations of a poet." Closer to our times, Robert Frost (1874-1963) speaks to the subject in these words: "Poetry is what is lost in translation." If in translating Shēms's poems into English, its intrinsic musicality—its tone, texture, and timbre—as well as other aspects of form have, inescapably, been altered or blocked, we still hope that something of their spirit has been imaginatively captured.

TRANSLITERATION

The transliteration system for Armenian used in this work is based on the scheme adopted by the Library of Congress (see: *Cataloging Service, Bulletin 121*, Spring, 1977). It follows the phonetic values of Classical and Eastern Armenian. However, wherever deemed useful, Western Armenian phonetic values have also been utilized. For ease of reading, I have in certain cases taken liberties, giving preference to speech sounds over the rules of transliteration, as in *astvats* and not *astowats* or *astuats* and *Gēvorg* and not *Gēorg*. I have also chosen to render the most prevalent Armenian name ending as *–ian* instead of *–yan* or *–ean*.

It is hoped that the present biography will not only open a window on Hmayeak Shēms's tempestuous life and poetic voice, but will also contribute to future studies of this important poet and man of letters.

Vahé Baladouni
Washington, DC
June 2009

Acknowledgments

For four months, following our evacuation from our ravaged home in New Orleans, my wife and I enjoyed the warm hospitality of our daughter, Janig Hokis Baladouni Heard, and son-in-law, Dru Patrick Heard, at their Falls Church, Virginia, residence, for which we express our gratitude. We also extend our deeply-felt thanks to our son, Vahan Baladouni, who was helpful in more ways than one during the days of our evacuation. Last, but not least, I am indebted to Anne and John Heard as well as Melissa McGuffee and Vidar Ludwigsen for their assistance in rescuing the surviving archive.

During the preparation of this biography, I have received helpful suggestions from Fr Krikor Maksoudian, student of Armenian culture; Levon Avdoyan, Armenian Area Specialist at the Library of Congress; Aram Arkun, historian; and Khachig Tölölian, editor of *Diaspora: A Journal of Transnational Studies*, to all of whom I extend my appreciation. My special thanks to the staff of the African and Middle Eastern Reading Room of the Library of Congress who facilitated my research on this book. I acknowledge and thank the editor of *Cross-Cultural Communications* for permission to make extensive quotations from Hmayyag Shems, *For the House of Torkom* (1999). Acknowledgment is also due, with thanks, to the editor of *Ararat Quarterly* for allowing me to reprint Gurgēn Mkhit'arian's memoir, "A Portrait of Hmayeak Shēms" (Spring 1999). As always, I thank my wife, Billie Salisbury Baladouni, whose loving support of my scholarly projects has made my work enjoyable.

On his part, John Gery wishes to acknowledge the Department of English at the University of New Orleans and the Institute for Advanced Study at the University of Minnesota-Minneapolis for allotting him time to work on this biography. He also wishes to thank Stanley Barkan, Editor/Publisher of

Cross Cultural Communications, for his commitment to making Hmayeak Shēms available to English readers, as well as to thank his wife, Biljana Obradovic, for her sustaining support of his work at translation. Lastly, John wants to give an especial tribute of gratitude to Vahé Baladouni for inviting him to participate in this valuable project and for teaching him so much about Armenian language, literature, and culture.

V.B.

Reference Key

The following abbreviations are used in the references to Shēms's works:

R   *Ṛoshnakan* [Luminous], 1943.
SN   *Sayat'-Nova: Matean imastut'ean, geghets'kut'ean ew anmatuyts' siroy* [Sayat-Nova: Book of Wisdom, Beauty, and Unrequited Love], 1944.
ĒE   *Ēntir Erker* [Select Works], 1994.
HT   For the House of Torkom, 1999.
PHG *Patmut'iwn hay grakanut'ean* [History of Armenian Literature], 2002.

A Chronology of Hmayeak Shēms

1896   Born 17 May in Gümüşhané, Turkey.
1909   Graduates from Surb Grigor Lusavorich' School (combined elementary and middle school) and enters Sanasarian Academy on full scholarship.
1912   Is expelled from Sanasarian Academy in February for his anarchistic activities.
1913   Graduates from the Diocesan Clerical College of Erevan and starts teaching at the Armenian School in Sukhumi, Georgia.
1915   Learns of the Armenian Genocide while living in Georgia.
1916   After the occupation of Trabzon by the Russian Army in April, rushes to his "parental hut" to find nothing but ashes. Lives the life of a wandering dervish throughout the Caucasus and Southern Russia for the next three years.
1919   Assumes a teaching position at the Armenian Orphanage in Trabzon.
1923   Arrives in Romania. Teaches at Armenian schools in Strunga and Constantsa. Publishes his early poems in *Navasard* and *Hrazdan* periodicals.
1924   Arrives in Egypt. After a few months in Cairo, moves to Alexandria and assumes a teaching position at Poghosian National School.
1927   Moves to Paris to study psychotherapy at Fondation Henri Durville.
1929   Returns to Alexandria to assume responsibility for his now widowed sister, Haykuhi Baladouni, who took up residence there

	with her family that same year. Practices psychotherapy for a year.
1930	Assumes teaching at Haykaznian Gymnasium and Palayan School.
1935	Is reappointed to teaching position at Poghosian National School.
1941-1942	Writes and delivers major lecture series on Armenian literature at Haykaznian Gymnasium.
1943	Publishes *Ṛoshnakan*, a collection of essays and poems.
1944	Publishes *Sayat'-Nova: Matean imastut'ean, geghets'kut'ean ev anmatuyts' siroy*, a study on the eighteenth-century minstrel, Sayat-Nova.
1948	Resumes teaching at Haykaznian Gymnasium. Speaks out in favor of repatriation, despite opposition to it from Dashnak Party.
1951	Continues literary translations into Armenian despite declining health.
1952	Dies on 30 March in Alexandria, Egypt, after being treated for a month at the Anglo-Swiss Hospital for alcoholism.

A Diasporan Journey: Cities Where Shēms Visited and Lived.

I

Student, Rebel, and Wandering Dervish: From Trabzon to the Caucasus and the Balkans

PROLOGUE: SHĒMS, THE DERVISH—
"THAT HAPLESS, TATTERED NOBLEMAN"[1]

When Hmayeak Shēms died in Alexandria, Egypt, on 30 March 1952, the Armenian press in the diaspora—across four continents, from Cairo to Boston, Buenos Aires to Paris, Beirut to Tehran—echoed the passing of a poet whose work has been aptly characterized as "the poetry of pure spirit."[2] Articles, memoirs, reminiscences, and testimonials commemorating the occasion appeared in Armenian language newspapers and periodicals, each in its own way shedding light on the many-faceted life of a man of letters who had lived most of his life as "a lone émigré in search of Mt Ararat and its shade."[3] Among the plethora of articles, an editorial in a Cairo-based newspaper, entitled "Mer Korustnerĕ" [Our Losses], captured Shēms's adult life in its stark reality:

> [Shēms was] a wandering minstrel, a troubadour, who for all appearances wasn't from this world and who gave more to life than life had given to him. . . . [He] fought against life practically every day, every hour, without ever fearing death, always toiling, always creating, and always serving the Word and Poetry. [He was] a modern-day monk who spent sleepless nights engaged in labor, with merely a wafer and a sip of water, and who had found the way to consider himself a Croesus even in his émigré existence.[4]

Half a world away, in Boston, the noted Armenian literary critic, Gurgēn Mkhit'arian (1890-1962), wrote in a portrayal of Hmayeak Shēms:

> Shēms's writing is the poetry of pure spirit, the murmur of a restless soul. It is a cry of protest and rebellion, a quest for beauty and a dream, expressed in a

powerful voice. His works include an array of prose and poetry, consisting of both original works and translations. It is, in short, unnecessary to label Shēms as orator, poet, journalist, teacher, or political activist. Quite simply, he was all these, with none overshadowing the others, but all integral, inspired, genuine, unique and dynamic. Any literary work that voiced the spirit, or instilled the spirit, was acceptable to him.

In these compressed lines, Mkhit'arian captures the distinctive quality of Shēms's voice whose haunting, melodious tone evokes an aura of spiritual energy.

It is the life and works of this lone émigré that we attempt to explore in these pages more than a half-century after his death and the recent republication of several of his works. Shēms's émigré existence started no sooner than the onset of the Armenian Genocide of 1915. Though he himself was spared the genocide perpetrated on his fellow Armenians by the Turks, the anguish created by the carnage had an indelible effect on him. The memory of one and a half million Armenian victims, including his parents, grandparents, brother and sister, who were put to death, followed him for the rest of his life. If, for instance, his wish for an unceremonious burial for himself was grounded partly in his natural sense of humility, it was also, in part, or even more so, a gesture of identification with the victims of the genocide whose bodies had had no consecration and had found no grave. In a telling poem, "Burial," composed in his youth, first published in 1923, later revised, Shēms entreats nothing less than the night itself to honor his request:

> O starless, moonless, silent, pure black night,
> Carry my corpse, dispose of it far from here,
> Somewhere it can't be found, removed from sight,
> Devoid of stars, where none can scorn or sneer.
>
> O please don't bury me near some craggy hill
> Where winds moan endlessly, weary with dread,
> Nor where each spring bright flowers might bloom still
> And loved ones come to visit with their dead.
>
> No, silent, pure black night, bear me from here
> To where my corpse can be interred in sand.
> Then flee, leaving no sigh, no song, no tear,
> Nor even a sprig to mark that barren land. (ĔE 86)

The somber imagery and tone of these very personal lines, expressing the poet's last wishes, reveal his deep-seated identification with the victims of the genocide. The word "sand" in line two of the last stanza alludes to the deserts of Deir el-Zor to where defenseless and terrorized Armenian women and children were driven only to be burned alive; the men had been killed earlier in their hometowns. The phrase, "nor even a sprig," in the last line evokes the unmarked graves of those victims. This immense expanse of land remains engraved in the Armenian psyche as the crypt of a once vibrant nation. Rather than shun that horror, Shēms asks, in effect, to be united with those who have been eradicated from history.

Ironically, however, for one who had sought neither praise nor glory in his life, after his death Shēms was instead honored with a national funeral, his coffin draped in the red, blue, and orange colors of the flag of the short-lived independent Republic of Armenia (1918-1920). In Alexandria, Egypt, whose Armenian community had for nearly three decades been animated by Shēms's presence in its cultural life, the anonymity he sought eluded him; the community decided to conduct a funeral with the full pomp and circumstance worthy of a great son.

The day after he died, on a sunny mid-afternoon, mourners filled the St Paul-St Peter Armenian Apostolic Church of Alexandria to capacity. The clergy and distinguished leaders of the community, members of the Armenian Revolutionary Federation (ARF), and cultural organizations, as well as school principals, faculty and upper class students from nearby private and community schools, filed into the church. Boy-scouts stood at attention on either side of the casket prominently placed at the center of the church. Wreaths encased the casket. Elegies were sung and read inside the church, and later eulogies were delivered in the alcove. From the church Shēms's former students then carried his casket on their shoulders for several blocks to Place St Catherine,[5] where it was placed on a horse-driven hearse. From there the caravan of mourners followed the procession to the Armenian cemetery at Chatby, a suburban area where Catholic, Greek, Syrian, Coptic, Protestant, Jewish, and Armenian cemeteries all stretch contiguously on what was then a vast plain. Additional eulogies followed at the graveside, and then, after a final bow, the mourners departed.

Shēms's grave, which has since been marked by a tombstone bearing the Armenian inscription, "Hmayeak Sap'rich'ian (Shēms), 1896-1952, Teacher and Poet," lies only a few hundred yards from the beautiful Mediterranean Sea, whose breakers burst into silvery bubbles in summer and whose billowing waves charge against the shores in winter.

Posthumously, two separate editions of Shēms's selected works have appeared. The first was published in 1994 under the editorship of Vahé Baladouni, Shēms's nephew and literary executor, by Baikar Publications (Watertown, Massachusetts), and the second in 2002 under the editorship of Henrik Bakhch'inian, philologist and director of the Eghishē Ch'arents' Museum of Literature and Art (MLA), in Erevan, Armenia. A third volume, containing a fairly large number of Shēms's poems that over the years had been set to music, were collected and published by the Ch'arents' MLA the year before. A two-year lecture series delivered by Shēms on Armenian literature at Haikaznian Gymnasium in 1941-1942, first published in Cairo's *Houssaper* [Husaber] *Daily* in serial form, were also collected in a volume and republished by the Ch'arents' MLA in 2002 under Bakhch'inian's editorship. The edition of the complete works of Sayat-Nova, edited by Bakhch'inian and published by the Ch'arents' MLA in 2003 under the title *Khagher* [Songs], includes Shēms's 1944 study of Nova's work, as well as his rendition of twenty of Nova's songs into Western Armenian. The volume itself is dedicated to Shēms's memory. Among other reprints of Shēms's works, mention must be made of his rendition of Khach'atur Abovian's "Haṛajaban *Verk' Hayastani*" [Preface to *Wounds of Armenia*] into Western Armenian as well as an article entitled *"Mets azg erek' mateanov—urvagits"* [Great Nation with Just Three Books: An Outline] both of which were included in a first-time edition of Abovian's original manuscript of *Verk' Hayastani, Voghb Hayrenasiri, Patmakan Vep* [Wounds of Armenia: Lamentation of a Patriot, A Historical Novel], edited by Gurgēn Gasparian and published by the Ch'arents' MLA in 2004.

GROWING UP IN TRABZON

Hmayeak Shēms, pen name of Hmayeak Grigor Sap'rich'ian, was born on 17 May 1896, in Gümüşhané, Turkey, a town nestled on the lofty Pontic mountain range some forty-five miles (83 km) south-south-west of Trabzon. At one time the town had a large Armenian population who, by occupation, were merchants, storekeepers, and craftsmen. However, in the early years of the twentieth century, due to emigration to Trabzon and other major cities, the town began losing its former status. By the end of the first decade of the century, the number of Armenians in Gümüşhané had dwindled to approximately 1200.[6] The region, also named Gümüşhané, boasted at one time of being home to several Armenian monasteries. However, the Turko-Mongol invasions of centuries past had decimated all but one, *Surb P'rkich' Vank'* [Monastery of Holy Savior], in the proximity of the town. Located in a picturesque setting and enjoying a healthy climate, the monastery also served as a summer resort for wealthy Trabzonians, as well as for pilgrims and sojourners.[7] In a rare recollection written about his boyhood years, Shēms quotes from a description of the natural ambiance of his birthplace he himself had penned in his younger days:

> My parental home was perched at the crest of a cliff, overhanging a deep valley. That was where my eyes first drank in the honey-colored sunlight. There the rocks glittered with silver and gold. There, in the recesses of dark caves, huddled gold ingots and priceless gems. The fragrant air of the mountains, which rushed in with exhilaration through my large window, was my constant playmate.[8]

However, before long Shēms's family moved from Gümüşhané to Trabzon. If the last half of his abbreviated life was to be spent on the shores of the Mediterranean in Alexandria, most of his earliest years were spent by the shores of the Black Sea, in a very different coastal city, Trabzon. Located some seven hundred sixty-one miles (1410 km) north-east of Alexandria, Trabzon is the capital of a province by the same name which lies on a wide bay on the southeastern shore of the Black Sea, backed by the high ranges of the Pontic Mountains. Historically known as Trapezus, it is believed to have been founded in 756 BCE by Greek colonists from Sinope, and throughout its long history, it has seen many conquerors come and go, including the Romans, Goths, Chaldeans, Byzantines, and Ottoman Turks. During Byzantine rule, Trapezus became the capital of the Empire of Trabzon (1204-1461). Finally, in 1461, it was annexed to the Ottoman Empire and today continues to remain part of its successor state, Turkey.

As a port near historical Armenia, Trabzon had during most of its history an Armenian population with a major concentration of merchants. At the time of Shēms's birth, the province numbered an Armenian population of approximately 65,000, while the city itself was home to nearly 6,000 Armenians.[9] It was in this historic city, between the roar of the Black Sea and a bustling Armenian community, that Shēms grew up:

> One day, I heard a frightful and endless song. Massive volumes of water were battering against the walls of our home. I was moved from the summit of a mountain to a new home by the sea. It was the sea that was singing. I loved that song. My childhood passed by the sea, listening to the music of the waves.[10]

The eldest of four children (two brothers and two sisters), Shēms grew up in a financially distressed home. His father, Grigor Sap'rich'ian (in Armenian *sap'rich'* means barber), a man of bright intellect, was by vocation a barber catering to the working-class and barely able to support his family of seven, which included not only his wife and four children, but also Shēms's paternal grandmother. Shēms's mother, T'urvanta Tserunian, a highly sensitive woman, was a homemaker. Aside from his parents' names and occupations, little else is known about Shēms's lineage. Despite what Shēms recalls about "the music of the waves," the family residence, writes Shēms's boyhood friend and classmate H. Arshakuni [pen name of Hovakim Hovakimian], was actually located "off a main street, on a passage way, in a basement apartment where the sun never shone."[11]

These dire conditions constituted Shēms's early life, yet the loving atmosphere in the family and very likely the natural beauty of the Pontus more than compensated for the material deprivation. We also know from Shēms's own remembrances that along with his parents' love and attention, he also enjoyed the undivided devotion of his grandmother. In great measure Shēms owed his love for Armenian literature to his blue-eyed grandmother who would recite to him long passages from it by heart. This same grandmother also knew how to stir and enchant young Shēms's imagination with incomparable fairy tales. Years later, Shēms would commit some of those tales to print, such as "Mardĕ vor Astvats gtav" [The Man Who Found God] (*ĒE* 216-224) and "Odzĕ barerar" [The Benefactor Snake] (*ĒE* 225-233), all written in the accents of legend. Fascinating in their conception and narrative power, the former concerns the theme of what people pray for and how God responds, and the latter, how an avaricious and miserly character named Abu Ahmed discovers his better—that is, his giving and generous—self.

As was customary in Shēms's time, children of Armenian descent started their schooling at the age of four. Shēms was registered at the Lusaworch'ian National School, a combined elementary and middle school. The Armenian word "lusaworch'ian" may be translated as "dispersion of light" or "dissemination of intellectual/spiritual light" or, simply, "illumination" or "enlightenment," though the specific reference here may well be to St Gregory the Illuminator, *Surb Grigor Lusaworich'* in Armenian, the revered champion of the Christian faith in Armenia.[12]

Shēms's classmate, Arshakuni, remembers Shēms as one of two bright students who occupied front row seats in the classroom. He describes Shēms as a youngster with "a full round face, deep-set eyes, aquiline nose, wide forehead, and hair always combed backward." He was familiarly known to his classmates as the school's "little poet" and received special attention from his Armenian teacher, Barunak Ter-Harut'iwnian, who encouraged his literary efforts. "Almost every day Shēms's poems would be the topic of a lesson," notes Arshakuni. He then adds: "He had a thick notebook of poems from which we, his classmates, liked to read out loud. But not satisfied with our reading, he would grab the notebook from our hands and, rising to his feet, recite them himself in his sonorous voice." Arshakuni also remembers how during school assemblies, alongside the works of other poets, Shēms recited from his own poetry, eliciting hearty applause. "What's more," he continues, "at the conclusion of these school assemblies, the school principal would come over to congratulate the little poet's parents, whose eyes would well up with tears of joy."[13]

Shēms's schoolmates also remember him as a sensitive, contemplative boy who did not engage in rough games; otherwise, he was very sociable. Whether alone or with companions, he would spend long hours on the docks watching the ships arrive and depart. One evening, relates Arshakuni, a group of Shēms's friends were at Avo's Hotel for a social evening when Shēms suddenly appeared, entering the room at a quick pace and visibly agitated. Earlier, while he had been strolling the harbor with Bagrat, one of his classmates, a group of French tourists had approached them for information. At first, they had singled out Bagrat for he was elegantly dressed.

But as his French was not adequate to answer the tourists' questions satisfactorily, Shēms's intervention had become necessary. However, as soon as Shēms had satisfied their queries, the tourists had turned back to Bagrat and asked him to lead the way. Offended by this incident, Shēms expressed his indignation at such human superficiality. He simply could not reconcile himself to the idea that people attach so much importance to external appearances.

These early life experiences, particularly the economic deprivation, left a mark on Shēms's impressionable mind. Indeed, over his relatively brief literary career, Shēms would find himself, again and again, driven to address social injustices in his essays and, not infrequently, from the podium.

A TURBULENT SECONDARY SCHOOL EDUCATION

It was a day of festivity! Dressed in their Sunday best, the graduating Class of 1909 at Lusaworch'ian National School basked in the June sunshine, celebrating the completion of their program of study. But one among them, Shēms, was quiet and in a pensive mood. The uncertainty of his future education weighed heavily on him. His parents were thinking of sending him to the local French school, but Shēms's own desire was to continue his studies at the celebrated Sanasarian Academy in Karin (Erzurum), some one hundred eighteen miles (218 km) south-south-west of Trabzon.[14] His parents' inclination to keep him at home was due partly to their modest means and partly to their extreme attachment to their son. But despite his mutual feeling for them, Shēms longed to challenge himself.

One evening, Shēms's teacher, Barunak Ter-Harut'iwnian, and his school principal, Sahak Ēt'mēk'chian,[15] came to visit his parents in order to persuade them to send their son to Sanasarian Academy. The two men explained that they had secured a sponsor for Shēms and that, if as parents they truly wished the best for their son, they must let him continue his education at Sanasarian. Still time passed. Shēms's parents simply could not come to a decision. Their pride would not allow them to accept financial assistance even for their child's education, nor could they reconcile themselves to the idea of being separated from their eldest son. Finally, in this atmosphere of uncertainty, Shēms's mother broke the impasse. Yielding to her son's silent entreaties, she rose to her feet, removed the modest jewelry she was wearing, and placed it on the table, saying, "I will not have my son deprived of attending the school of his choice." Years later, Shēms would often recall the simple majesty of that scene.

Later, in August, a group of five graduates from Lusaworch'ian, including Shēms and Arshakuni, set out for Karin in the company of their teacher, Ter-Harut'iwnian,[16] who was himself a graduate of Sanasarian Academy.

"It was not without some difficulty that we were admitted to the Academy's third grade," writes Arshakuni. "However," he adds, "the results we achieved in the mid-term examinations justified the consideration shown toward us. Our group of boys from Trabzon turned out to rank among the best students in the class, while Shēms emerged as the top student in all subjects."[17] Here, as in Lusaworch'ian, Shēms's writing soon earned him the title of "school poet." His poems were published in the Academy's collotype monthly, *Sirt* [Heart]. Also here, as at Lusaworch'ian, he was called upon to recite his poetry at school assemblies. Shēms, who had been enticed to Armenian and world literature from his earliest school days, continued his relentless reading at Sanasarian, availing himself of the Academy's rich library of Armenian and French language books.

After completing his first year at Sanasarian, Shēms returned home to Trabzon to spend the summer with his family. Unbeknownst to him, it was to be his last visit with his loved ones, except for his sister, Haykuhi, who miraculously survived the Armenian Genocide of 1915 and later took refuge in Egypt. In a memoir, Shēms recalls how during that summer he and his friends had the distinct privilege of meeting three major Armenian political figures: the novelist Avetis Aharonian (1866-1948), the poet Avetik' Isahakian (1875-1957), and the sociologist Garegin Khazhak (1867-1915).[18] Aharonian and Khazhak had received their university education in Europe, had occupied top-level offices in the ARF, and had held editorial assignments in leading Armenian newspapers. Five years later, Khazhak was to become yet another victim of the Genocide. Aharonian, as a delegate of the newly born Armenian Republic, would be a signatory to the Treaty of Sèvres (10 August 1920) in Paris. Isahakian, a lyric and epic poet as well as short-story writer, would continue to live in various European cities until his return home to Soviet Armenia in 1936 where he earned for himself the title of "master." But in the summer of 1910 the "Great Three," as Shēms calls them, were traveling together, coming from Karin to Trabzon on a speech-making tour.

One evening, as Shēms and his friends were relaxing at the ARF Cultural Club, much to their surprise, they saw the "Great Three" walk in. There was great excitement in having the three leading intellectual figures in their midst. Though a large crowd gathered around them, the "Great Three" showed special interest in the students from Sanasarian. During conversation, one of Shēms's loquacious friends, pointing to him, said: "Are you aware, comrades, that this one here writes poetry?" Shēms blushed, but all three demanded that he show them his writings. He could hardly refuse; though he was certainly intimidated by the honor bestowed him. The following day, with a quivering hand he copied out a few of his poems and with two or three friends headed to the home of the Tiraturians, a prominent family of the Trabzon community with whom the "Great Three" were staying.

The "Great Three" were indeed expecting him. The two Avos, as Shēms labels them (Avo short for Avetis and Avetik'), got down to business immediately, each reading the poems in turn and making comments. Shēms and his friends listened, hanging on their every word. Then Khazhak, who had just woken up from his early afternoon siesta, entered the room and roared in his husky voice: "Hey, you dummies, why are you showing your poems to them? Each of them belongs to a literary school. I am a man of science. Only I can deliver an impartial opinion." The two Avos laughed and said: "You can have your say, too; there's still time to speak." Following this exchange, continues Shēms in his memoir, they talked among themselves in Russian, "which in those days none of us students understood." Finally, looking up from the scrutinized pages before him, Isahakian turned to Shēms and announced: "When Vahan Tērian sent me his book of poems,[19] I mentally crossed him off as a poet; but see what a great poet he turned out to be. What I mean is that our words aren't worth much. Follow your own course and you'll go far." Reflecting on the "Great Three," Shēms adds:

> From that day on our three great comrades became my three mentors. Aharonian has been for me the master of a warm and melodious style. With his *Songs and Wounds,* Isahakian has kept me under the spell of Armenian folklore and brought me down from Parnassus. And Khazhak has opened my eyes to the broad horizons of social life and its patterns of development. The advice all three offered me was *to live the life of my people and to write for my people.* [Italics added.]

Shēms abided by this motto throughout his own troubled life and times.

Soon that memorable summer came to an end, and Shēms returned to Karin, to his cherished academy. The school buildings, recollects Arshakuni, were encircled by fortress-like walls, with only two connecting points to the outside world: one was under the constant watch of a gatekeeper, and the other was always kept locked except on Sundays, when it was opened to conduct rows of students to church and back again. Although the school provided excellent intellectual nourishment, its isolation from the outside world coupled with its strict rules and the control exercised over the students' minds, had begun to make them feel like birds in a golden cage. Thus they eagerly awaited the advent of summer when they could pack up their belongings and move to the Academy's summer camp in nearby Srtadzor [Valley of the Heart]. For a while the students could forget the strictures of school life and commune with nature.

However, this interlude also had its drawbacks. When they returned to campus, they found the atmosphere there more restrictive than ever, and the school's confines and discipline stirred them to unrest. Now in their mid-teens, Shēms and some of his schoolmates found the school's environment too oppressive to their young spirits, as their flights of fancy collided with rigid regulations. It was no surprise, then, that an anarchistic mood soon developed and grew increasingly public in its expression. According to Arshakuni, finally a group of approximately twenty students organized themselves to stage a protest. They held secret meetings and set up their own private library, with Friedrich Nietzsche's works occupying a central place.

As one of the group's most active members, Shēms soon immersed himself in Nietzsche's writings, in particular *Thus Spake Zarathustra*, and could recite passages from it by heart. Moreover, he adopted Nietzsche's literary style in both his writing and his speech. This group of disgruntled students increasingly dominated the school's inner life, demonstrating signs of insubordination. Before long, the school's administration decided to put a quick end to this movement, and Shēms, as its most articulate spokesperson, became the first victim. Halfway through the academic year, in February 1912, Shēms was expelled from the Academy. "This had an enormous impact on the group," writes Arshakuni, "and his like-minded friends protested to the administration. I myself made impassioned appeals. But principal Khach'atrian called me into his office and threatened to expel me, too, if I did not cease my involvement." A few months after Shēms's departure, however, the Academy's Board of Trustees, in response to the activities of the anarchists, was forced to suspend classes for nearly two months, and ultimately they shut down the school, leaving behind an entire student body labeled as "insubordinates."[20] Some months later, the Academy reopened its doors in a new location in the city of Sebastia (Sivas), one hundred ninety-two miles (356 km) west of Karin. However, the institution never fully recovered from this "anarchistic" blow, and by 1914, it completely closed down.

Shēms was not quite sixteen years old when he was expelled from the prestigious Sanasarian Academy. Whether the harsh penalty meted out to this idealistic youngster was in truth the best decision for all concerned matters little. Shēms was victimized for espousing an ideology that ran counter to the traditional values of the school administration. At the risk of stating the obvious, we must ask: could not Shēms see the writing on the wall? Despite his relative immaturity he surely must have seen the potential consequences of his outspoken behavior. Why, then, did he not compromise? Here, too, the answer is easy to imagine: he held his intellectual freedom above all else. Indeed, his entire life bears witness to his remarkable level of integrity and independence of mind.

In the early decades of the twentieth century, at least in certain circles, Nietzsche was, more often than not, seen as a voice akin to Socrates, a voice thought to corrupt the young. Those who loved and followed Nietzsche were quickly labeled as dissidents or anarchists. In many quarters, these labels were tantamount to the more provocative term of "socialists." Whatever the label, followers of Nietzsche were considered enemies of existing institutions and beliefs. While Nietzsche's *Zarathustra* with its proclamation of the death of God and concomitant call to revalue all values is indeed a powerful critique of Western culture, unfortunately in the eyes of many it obscured the more positive ideals written into this philosophical poem, among the most imaginative pieces of European literature. On the latter count, by the time Shēms read him in 1911 or 1912, Nietzsche had already made himself attractive to a wide range of creative thinkers and artists in the West, from George Bernard Shaw to Sigmund Freud. Most notably, he was also the hero of a generation of Armenian intellectuals and poets, such as Daniel Varuzhan (1884-1915) and Vahan Terian (1875-1920).

For Shēms, *Zarathustra* was a metaphysical masterpiece, thoroughly imbued with moral and, in its broadest sense, religious tenets, upholding the ideal of the *Übermensch*, the "higher human." As a rebellious spirit himself, Shēms spoke out not only for independence of mind, but also for personal liberation from all creeds. Yet, despite his emphasis on individual self-fulfillment, Shēms recognized along with Nietzsche that the full realization of one's humanity is irrevocably linked to the creative appropriation of tradition. Nevertheless, to the administrators of Sanasarian Academy, the very names of Nietzsche and Zarathustra, often used interchangeably, were simply a threat to the established order of things. Still, from those secondary school days to the end of his life, Shēms remained a true Nietzschean, loathing decadence of all types and struggling with fierce energy against it. Those who have known Shēms would attest along with Mkhit'arian that

> [whenever] someone raised a disturbing or distressing public concern, or alluded to the vanity of the rich and famous or those in authority and positions of power, then [Shēms's] face would flush and twist and bend in contortions; his tone would become stern and prolonged, his scowl like lightning, his words harsh.

Throughout his life Shēms remained fiery and passionate on social justice issues. His brief but sagacious articles and essays, such as "Mer zhamanaknerě" [Our Times] (*ĔE* 278-280), and "Vripats k'aghak'akrt'ut'iwn mě" [An Aborted Civilization] (*ĔE* 257-259), underscore the ills that have plagued human society and the urgent need for their overhaul.

If, on the one hand, Shēms wrote and spoke in Nietzschean style, he was, on the other hand, equally immersed in Buddhism, finding important correspondences between the two philosophies.[21] As a person, Shēms was a Spartan, an ascetic. In this sense, the Buddhist vision of spiritual self-realization guided him to the end. He believed that detaching himself from worldly things could enable him to attain peace and thus approach a state of nirvana. His innermost outlook on his own life is powerfully depicted in the following lines from his prose poem, "The Dervish" (1939):

> From one place to another he wanders, at best wrapped in a deerskin and carrying a bowl for alms, with an endless string of prayer beads dangling from his fingers. He carries all his belongings with him . . . he has no reason to look back, no reason for regret. (*HT* 33)

As a dervish, he saw himself in the lone figure of a man

> pass[ing] with an air of disdain through our cluttered streets of needs and lusts . . . . dispens[ing] his evanescent smile of privation on every opulence and luxury he sees, and even on more modest needs; he pities all that he beholds, then passes on. Free and at peace within himself, he beholds the disorder of our world and, instead of lamenting, sounds his call to our perplexed souls. (*HT* 35)

In this light, Nietzsche and Buddha represent the two opposing sides of Shēms's character—a rebellious spirit on public issues on the one hand, yet a young man of peace and dervish-like self-containment, on the other.

HEADING FOR ĒJMIATSIN AND EREVAN

After his expulsion from Sanasarian Academy, Shēms did not return home to his parents. With only a notebook of poems under his arm and a small bundle of clothes on his back, the sixteen-year-old "anarchist" headed east to Ējmiatsin in the bitter cold winter of 1912. Since its establishment over seventeen centuries ago, Ējmiatsin, some one hundred thirty-six miles (252 km) east of Karin, has served as the spiritual and administrative center of the Armenian Apostolic Church. There, Shēms applied to Gēvorgian Academy. Established in 1874, the Academy had in earlier years served as a school for training teachers and for preparing men for the priesthood. But by the turn of the twentieth century, it had developed into a strong liberal arts college with a major emphasis on Armenian studies.[22]

Shēms's application to the Academy was, however, denied, since he had applied too far along in the school year. But having secured a letter of recommendation from Ējmiatsin, Shēms then traveled another twelve miles (22 km) eastward to Erevan, where in September 1912, he took the Diocesan Clerical College's entrance examination and was accepted into the senior class. During the academic year 1912-1913, Shēms also found a paying position in the Diocesan offices. Owing to his intellectual gifts and modesty, he soon won the respect and affection of both faculty and staff, and before long he enjoyed the patronage of Bishop Khorēn Muratbēkian, Primate of the Erevan Diocese, who was later conferred the title archbishop and in 1933 was elected Kat'oghikos of All Armenians. Kat'oghikos Khorēn I served in that capacity until his mysterious death in 1938.[23]

In his senior year, Shēms was privileged to have as his teacher and friend Arsēn Tērtērian (1882-1953), a scholar and literary critic who, in 1943, would be elected to the Academy of Sciences of the Armenian SSR as founding member. In the 1920s, Tērtērian, along with such renowned scholars as Manuk Abeghian and Hrach'ya Acharian, was instrumental in developing a world-class program of study in Armenian Literature and Language at the Erevan State University. At the time of Shēms's attendance at the Diocesan Clerical College, Tērtērian had already established a reputation as a literary critic. His 1910 monograph on the poet Vahan Tērian (1885-1920) had made him an idol in the eyes of aspiring young writers. Tērian's own first collection of poems, *Mt'nshaghi Anurjner* [Twilight Reveries] (1908), the same volume mentioned by Avetik' Isahakian in his encounter with Shēms's poetry a few years earlier, had endeared him to the reading public, mainly due to its musicality which evokes a sense of homesickness, love, loss, death and transience. While recognizing this haunting musicality in Tērian's poetry, Tērtērian's critique did not fail to emphasize Nietzsche's influence on him.[24]

In one of his rare memoirs, Shēms describes himself at age sixteen going to visit Tērtērian, who had invited him to his home to discuss his writings. As we know now, this meeting with Tērtērian proved to be of crucial significance in Shēms's life:

> One Sunday morning in January 1913, as the snow was gently falling over the city of Erevan, . . . a young man clad in a heavy overcoat, unbuttoned, with a parcel under his arm, went rushing through the streets to keep an appointment. . . . That day, I was that young man; I was going to meet with my teacher and friend, Arsēn Tērtērian. He had honored me by inviting me to his home to discuss my writings.
>
> At the entrance to Tērtērian's home, I stopped for a moment, wiped the sweat from my forehead, and at last rapped at the door. A brown-skinned elderly woman of medium height opened the door:
>
> "Is Mr Tērtērian here?"
>
> "Yes, won't you come in?"
>
> She led me to the study, which I found warm and intimate. The *pechka* (печка)—an iron brazier built into the wall—was crackling noisily, taking delight in its red flames . . . No sooner had we settled comfortably into our chairs, when Tērtērian began reading the dozen or so pieces I had delivered to him.
>
> After a while, the kindly housekeeper interrupted us with tea. By then, Tērtērian was almost finished reading. Soon, looking me in the eye, he broke

into a smile and said: "Well, my boy, it seems you are going to become a teacher." I had indeed chosen that hallowed profession for myself. So I responded quickly: "Yes, Mr. Tērtērian; but who told you?" "Your writings tell me; it seems you are so concerned with not being understood that it stirs a fear in you, and that fear makes a person a teacher—often, I must add, to the detriment of his art."

It would be no exaggeration to say that this verdict created first dizziness, then an emptiness in my skull. But I collected myself and asked: "Do you see the influence of any author on my writings?" "Yes," he replied, "Vahan Tērian's." At that moment a protracted groan rose from the depths of my being: No! No! I want to be myself, just myself. Then a guffaw, followed by explosive laughter, erupted from Tērtērian's corner: "O, great! You really have done a wonderful thing," I heard Tērtērian say. In my moment of anger I had thrown all my writings—poems and prose—into the *pechka*, and they were now blazing into ashes as they shot up in beautiful flames. Tērtērian then continued: "You did well, that's a good sign; you wish to find your true self, to create your own voice and image, and therein lies your real worth as an artist."[25]

Soon after this episode, Shēms, the one labeled by faculty and administrators at Sanasarian Academy as Nietzschean and, moreover, who saw himself as Nietzschean, asked Tērtērian how he distinguished between the two styles of writing—the Nietzschean and the Tērianesque—to which Tērtērian replied: "Among us Armenians, the Nietzschean style of writing is intricately linked to the rhetoric of Tērian; therefore, you, sir, belong to Tērian's school." Indeed, Tērian's musicality influenced the lyricism of Shēms's early poems, a lyricism he never abandoned.

FIRST TEACHING APPOINTMENT

After graduating from the Diocesan Clerical College of Erevan in Spring 1913, Shēms left Armenia for the first time in his life to join the faculty of the Armenian School in Sukhumi, Georgia, two hundred twenty-eight miles (422 km) north of Erevan, as a first-grade teacher. As a general rule, the school's administration did not entrust the instruction of first-grade Armenian language to beginning teachers. However, the principal, Mat'evos Darbinian (1889-1941), had honored Shēms by turning one of the concurrent classes of the first grade Armenian language over to him, now but seventeen years old.

During this first year of his teaching career, it happened that the regional school inspector, Hovhannes Ter-Mirak'ian (1856-1938), paid an official visit and sat in on the young teacher's Armenian class. Following his observation, Ter-Mirak'ian entered his comments in a special register maintained for that purpose. The register was at the disposal of the Board of Trustees and faculty alike. In his comments, the school inspector severely criticized Shēms because three, out of a class of some thirty-seven students, had incorrectly accented the word "hankarts" [suddenly, in English]. Instead of placing the accent on the last syllable, as is customary in Armenian and pronouncing it "hanka´rts," they had accented the first syllable, "ha´nkarts." After reading Ter-Mirak'ian's critique, Shēms sought him out and resorted to wit in response to the criticism. In his memoir, Shēms recalls with bittersweet nostalgia the instructive exactitude of the inspector's remark:

> One would think that the very house of the Armenian nation had fallen apart on account of this. During those days of my youth, I may have taken the matter lightly. And I joked with him, saying that placing the accent on the first syllable stemmed from the very essence of that word, that it would be entirely appropriate to recite "ha´nkarts" instead of "hanka´rts." But he just smiled and suggested that the accents be put in their proper places.[26]

This episode from Shēms's early teaching career was later often invoked in his literary gatherings to underscore the attitude he believed every educated Armenian should hold toward the "medsask'anch'," literally meaning "the most splendid." As a term of endearment associated with the Armenian language, this expression has several unwritten connotations, such as *the most celebrated, the distinguished, the illustrious, the majestic, the sacred, and the sublime,* calling attention to the high regard in which Armenians hold their language. In his testimonial, written after Shēms's death, Step'an Shahpaz remembers how Shēms "doted on and cared for [every word and sentence] as if they were his own children."[27] As much as he gave himself to the musical quality of the Armenian language, Shēms was equally devoted to using words precisely, clearly. In both regards he held Armenian as nothing less than a sacred trust.

THE DAY THE SUN DARKENED: THE ARMENIAN GENOCIDE OF 1915[28]

To understand the true shock and depth of the impact of the Armenian Genocide—not only on Shēms, but on all Armenians—it is necessary to have at least a general sense of the long history of Armenia.[29] As in all horrific cases of genocide, the destruction of huge populations shatters much more than the lives, communities, and social values of those immediately involved. Indeed, genocide is a deliberate attempt to eradicate a people's past and future as well as their present, an act of obliterating an entire culture.

The origins of the Armenian people can be traced as far back as the middle of the second millennium BCE. Historically, Armenia covers a vast expanse estimated at 116,000 sq mi (300,000 sq km), approximately the size of modern-day Poland, between coordinates 37° and 49° East longitude and 37.5° and 41.5° North latitude, set on a plateau ranging from 3,300 to 6,600 feet high, a land mass often viewed as a "landlocked island." However, the presence of lofty mountains, averaging in altitude from 9,900 to 13,200 feet, with the Pontus range to the north, the Taurus to the south, and other ranges to the southeast, give this land yet the look of a "fortress." The biblical rivers, the Euphrates and the Tigris, which run from north to south emptying conjointly into the Persian Gulf, originate in these rugged mountains. Here, these rivers are actually mountain torrents rushing through all-but-inaccessible canyons. A third river, the Araxes, flows from west to east to join the Kura, before emptying into the Caspian Sea. On the heart of this land rises Mount Ararat (*Masis* in Armenian; altitude: 16,696 ft) with its eternally snow-capped peak, on whose summit once rested Noah's Ark, as biblical history has it.

However, this lofty, "fortress-like" land of Ararat (in much of recent Armenian historiography, "Ararat" is often used as a metaphor for Armenia) has been far from safe and secure over most of its history. Falling prey to the ambitions of militarily superior neighboring powers, Armenia has, through the centuries, served as a theater for savage wars. Only for brief periods has it enjoyed peace and stability. Yet despite its often bleak and turbulent history, it has enjoyed thriving commercial and cultural relations with other civilizations. Time and again, its creative people have sprung up to transform their tribulations into abiding works of art: architectural monuments, literary texts, painting, sculpture, and music. Though these works are the products of individual creative minds, they nevertheless express a trans-individual world, for they address the people's psychic needs. This rich cultural heritage has illuminated the path of the Armenian people through the hardships and contingencies of history.

In more recent times, Armenia was ravaged successively by the Seljuk Turks (mid-1000 to the 1240s), the Mongols (1240s to the 1380s) and the Turko-Tartar hordes led by Tamerlane, a Turkicized Mongol, from the 1380s on. These invasions caused unprecedented destruction and death, reducing Armenia to rubble. With the Ottoman capture of Constantinople in 1453, Armenia was cut off from Europe altogether. The rise of the Ottoman Empire (c1300-1922) to the west and the establishment of the powerful Safavid Dynasty (1502-1736) in neighboring Persia to the east set the stage for yet another long and brutal rivalry, as Armenia once again became a military borderland between these two powers. The incessant wars that followed, waged at the foot of Mount Ararat, forced Armenians to flee, resulting in the creation of new diaspora communities. In 1604, violating the 1590 treaty with the Ottoman Empire, Shah Abbas of Persia again invaded the Ottoman domains in South Caucasia. During this protracted campaign the Shah forcibly moved the Armenian population from Caucasian Armenia to Persia proper, leaving behind scorched cities and villages.

With Abdul-Hamid II's ascension to the Ottoman throne in 1878, hostility between Turks and Armenians only intensified. Abdul-Hamid, who later came to be known as the "Red Sultan" for his atrocities, suspended the constitution and initiated autocratic rule. By the last decade of the nineteenth century, as Western Armenians were articulating their own program for political, social, and economic reform, a paranoid Abdul-Hamid, anticipating the collapse of his realm, unleashed many massacres, including the Armenian massacre of 1895-1896, sending approximately 100,000 Armenians to their death and forcing survivors to convert to Islam. Twelve years later in 1908, however, Abdul-Hamid himself was deposed by insubordinate Army officers and exiled to Salonika (Thessaloniki, Greece). Following his departure, a new regime, known as the Young Turk regime, assumed power. This regime was welcomed enthusiastically as it offered the prospect of a Christian-Muslim brotherhood. But the optimism did not last long. By 1915, Turkish chauvinism re-emerged with an agenda of a meticulously planned, systematic genocide of the Armenian people throughout the former Ottoman Empire. The first genocide of the twentieth century was now under way in full force.

Shēms was still in Sukhumi, Georgia, on the same teaching assignment, teaching first-graders, when the bloody news of the Turkish atrocities reached him: *Armenians by the hundreds of thousands systematically and brutally murdered*. Word spread that males age ten and above in the Trabzon region were being rounded up, loaded into boats, taken out to the open sea, and ruthlessly thrown overboard. Women and children were being driven virtually in herds into the scorching, endless roads of the desert. Molested and tortured on the way, they were finally put to death, while their murderers looted and destroyed their homes and churches. In those days, there was not even an English word to describe accurately the annihilation of one and a half million Armenians living in the Ottoman Empire. It had to wait until the early 1940s for a Polish-born jurist, Raphael Lemkin, to coin the term "genocide" to describe the deliberate and systematic destruction of a people because of their religion or race.

THE AFTERSHOCK

As for so many others removed from the Armenian homeland, the horror of these mass massacres and deportations engulfed Shēms in untold, unfathomable ways. His beloved nation was in the throes of death, on the verge of annihilation. Shēms, whose very life was buttressed by the culture and traditions of the Armenian people, now found himself stripped of not only his physical, but also his spiritual home. It was as though his very soul had been taken from him. While the ultimate Turkish goal—the annihilation of the entire Armenian nation—inevitably failed, it succeeded, agonizingly to say, in sending a million and a half Armenians to their deaths. Among them were Shēms's parents, grandparents, brother, and one sister. Only his second sister, Haykuhi, was miraculously spared, as she took refuge in the home of a Greek family in Trabzon and later emigrated to Egypt. When, in an effort to occupy Ottoman Armenia, the Russian Army drove into Trabzon in April 1916, Shēms immediately returned to his "old parental hut." Some twenty years later, reliving that moment, Shēms would write in his "Erg haverzhakan" [Eternal Song]:

> You ripped from me abruptly every happy moment of life, O Lord!
> With barely a trace of mustache above my lip, a miserable pilgrim
> I became, when you drew me home again to my old parents' hut
> To find nothing to embrace but ashes and my bitter fate. (ĒE 52-53)

The sheer scope of the genocide cast a long, dark shadow over the survivors. Shēms himself, who had not yet turned twenty, fell into a spiritual exile as a sense of homelessness permeated his days and nights, rendering his life utterly meaningless. After a brief stay in Trabzon, he departed for Russia and the Caucasus, adopting the ways of a wandering dervish. From Sukhumi to Tzaretsin (present-day Volgograd), from Kerch to Rostov, and from Batum to Tiflis, he entered all levels of society, living among them, yet always retaining his individual values, or as Kipling would have said, living as a commoner among kings, and being virtuous in the crowd. Yet his unending exile exacted its toll; it was during this period that Shēms developed a habit of heavy drinking, which in time became excessive and, ultimately, undermined his health.

During those years Shēms was also into gambling, writes Arshakuni. On one such occasion, while playing a game of cards with Arshakuni's brother in Russia, Shēms lost four thousand rubles to him. Upon hearing of Shēms's loss, Arshakuni, who apparently served as his brother's custodian, secretly returned the entire sum to Shēms. Later, when Arshakuni's brother learned about it, he became furious; he even threatened "to kill" Shēms, if he refused to pay the money back. But fate intervened, and before long these two diametrically opposed individuals became inseparable friends. Some time later, when Arshakuni asked his brother if he had recovered his money from Shēms, he replied: "How can you ask for money from a man who is ready to give you his very last kopek?"[30]

In this same period, the Bolshevik revolution had reached the Caucasus. In 1918, a befuddled and weary Shēms took refuge in Tiflis. From there he traveled eighty miles (148 km) south to Erevan where he found the vast Western Armenian refugee population assembled on Eastern Armenia's indefinite borders. Famine and epidemic prevailed throughout the land. A year or so later, in the spring of 1919, Shēms backtracked, with a group of Armenian compatriots, to Batum, Georgia. "During those days," writes one of the group, Ervand Fntk'ian, "a majestic beard adorned Shēms's sallow cheeks. He had the same expressive eyes he had always had. Dressed carelessly, he joked sardonically." Fntk'ian then continues: "Only a handful of Armenian youths from Trabzon had survived the Genocide. Everyone was obsessed with crazy notions—thoughts of a just restitution—and Shēms was among those who kindled such thoughts. In the course of just a few years, Shēms, once well known as a modest, shy, serious poet, had undergone a complete transformation."[31]

Later that year Shēms returned to his ruined hometown, Trabzon, where, through the initiative of Garegin Vardapet Khach'aturian,[32] an orphanage had been opened, providing for the maintenance and education of some hundred and fifty surviving boys and girls. There, Shēms was asked to teach Armenian and mathematics. "As a teacher," attests Archbishop Khach'aturian, "Shēms knew how to make his classes lively and to win the hearts of his students." Elsewhere in his letter, written after Shēms's death, he comments: "[Shēms] was modest. He sought neither praise nor glory. Whatever he saw in himself as meritorious satisfied him. He shied away from sophistry and artificial decorum. He preferred simplicity, which was so unerring both in his person and in his apparel."[33]

Gurgēn Ter-Vardanian, a one-time colleague of Shēms at the orphanage, has also recollected those years:

> With his splendid beard, fur hat, and long overcoat Shēms created the impression of a real dervish. But his appearance was not all that pleasing to the Turks who, more than a dervish, saw in him the shade of an Armenian revolutionary. Nonetheless, Shēms was well versed in Turkish politics and was diplomatic in all his dealings with them. He merely befriended those who looked upon him with suspicion.

Elsewhere in his memoir, he underscores Shēms's ascetic life:

> Sometimes a group of us, teachers and students, would visit the decimated Armenian cemetery and monastery. Shēms joined us on those trips in a rather perfunctory way. He preferred to stay home, that is, in his rented room, engaged in his own thoughts and feelings. Social life in Trabzon was non-existent in those days. The once vibrant Armenian community of some five thousand now consisted of only a few hundred refugees and the orphanage.

He then continues:

> On occasion, the faculty would gather for tea or dinner at the Primate's home and discuss national and literary issues. At one such gathering we were

An ascetic Shēms. Trabzon, Turkey, c. 1921.

photographed at the request of the primate. The result was an astonishing, mysterious-looking image of Shēms looking like a monk, buried deep in his reading of *Narek*."[34]

In unfettered language, Ter-Vardanian captures young Shēms's most telling characteristics as a dervish, a revolutionary, a recluse, and a man-of-letters. These dimensions of his character would resurface much later in his writing, time and time again.

A REUNION OF SURVIVORS

With the closing of the Trabzon orphanage in December 1922, the entire student body was moved to Greece under the auspices of the Near East Relief Agency. By now elevated to the rank of bishop, Khach'aturian requested that Shēms accompany the youngsters to Greece and continue his work with them there. For some reason, however, the plan never materialized. Upon his arrival in Constantinople, Shēms continued directly to Romania, where for six months he taught at the Armenian orphanage of Strunga. For the following academic year, 1923-1924, he held a similar position at the Armenian community school in Constantsa.

Not far from Constantsa, an older schoolmate of Shēms, Vardan Gēvorgian, had settled in Varna, Bulgaria. "My post-war meeting with Shēms," writes Gēvorgian in his memoir, "took place in Constantsa in 1923. Shēms had invited me to meet with him and a few other survivors from Trabzon. I accepted." Gēvorgian then gives a vivid description of that meeting:

> Our meeting was highly emotional. The longing for the old days, the tragic fate of an entire generation exterminated in the hands of the Turks, and the need for a handful of survivors to console each other had, of course, become the reason for this gathering. That very same evening, a reception table was set up in a modest room.
>
> Shēms, with his abundant black beard, expressive eyes, and vibrating essence was, of course, there. There, too, were Misak T'orlak'ian, Pierre Mik'ayelian and, if my memory serves me right, Aram Erkanian, a native of Karin, who had joined us owing to his friendship with T'orlak'ian. After all, the Armenian Genocide had closed the distance between Trabzon and Karin, making this region an inseparable part of the historic Armenian homeland. There were rounds of toasts, heart-filled salutes, shared memories of the past, and warm conversation. For the first time I noticed that each time Shēms raised his glass of cognac he downed it to the bottom, finding this drink the most agreeable of liquors. It was not until the wee hours of the morning that we parted.

The next day the two old friends enjoyed a tête-à-tête at a waterfront café:

> The next day Shēms came to my hotel and led me to a waterfront café perched along the coast of the Black Sea in an area often referred to as the Romanian Riviera. At this café, with its distinctly western European cultural flair, we talked intimately and at length about the carnage, the horrendous massacres of the Armenians in Trabzon, and the young so full of promise and noble dreams, treacherously slaughtered by the bloodthirsty enemy. Shēms was deeply tormented. Being more familiar than I with the recent tragedy that had befallen the Armenian nation, and imbued with the monstrosities that had shaped our destiny, Shēms was writhing in anguish. As one who had been in Trabzon most recently, he related heart-rending accounts of the massacres. The city had lost its vibrant character. For a time, the Turks had shown some signs of taking responsibility for the inhuman acts of carnage they had committed, but that had lasted only a short time.

We then reflected upon the magnitude of the loss and the remnants.

> The Black Sea was calm now. It awakened so many memories in our minds, for we had both spent much time in our youth wandering its shores and dreaming. The sea had a singular appeal for us. Enraptured, we gazed at it while at the same time turning our conversation to our uncertain future.[35]

In its narrative as well as its tone, Gēvorgian's memoir conveys well not only how profoundly the genocide had traumatized Shēms's generation in every aspect of their lives, but also the degree to which the trauma left them without clear goals, almost aimless in trying to conduct their lives with some kind of normalcy for years to come. Indeed, some survivors, such as the eminent musicologist-ethnologist Komitas Vardapet,[36] were never able to recover.

A VOICE FROM THE DEPTHS OF THE SOUL

Eight years had gone by since the bloody news of the Turkish atrocities against its Armenian population had reached Shēms. Yet its impact on him had hardly diminished. The trauma of the genocide had inflicted such a deep emotional and spiritual wound that he felt his very life was under threat. An unspeakable, terrifying, and incomprehensible act of violence had been committed against him with the brutal death of his parents, brother, sister, the community, and a million and a half of his kith and kin. This traumatic wound had brought him to the brink of nihilism. Today, we know that the healing of a trauma cannot even begin until the circumstances of one's life are dramatically reversed, and even then only as part of a lifelong process. Indeed, the story of Shēms's life remains an example of this devastating experience of trauma.

In his prose poem entitled "Orphan," we catch a glimpse of the overwhelming effect the genocide had on the young Shēms. This piece, not written until 1938, brings out Shēms's paradigmatic identity poignantly:

> In my dream I cried a long time. I cried all night. All night I clutched to my breast a small child, frostbitten but with soulful blue eyes.

He then continues:

> An orphan, he had been much too long in the cold. I wanted to warm him up so he might withstand the bitter weather a little better.
>
> Gazing at me with a sweet yet doleful smile, he managed—between murmurs, coughs and spittle—to tell me his magical tale hoping that I might stop crying.
>
> He said he was an orphan who had come a long way. He lifted his tired feet, caked with thick clods of earth.
>
> *The roads were cold*, he explained. *Doors and windows were slammed in my face. Everywhere I was a stranger.*
>
> No one would take him in. As he stumbled along, they mocked him in his hunger and thirst.
>
> Then, to douse the fire of his thirst and diminish the specter of his hunger, they beat him with sticks.
>
> Through tearful eyes, I watched him looking at me with a smile as he whispered his odyssey.
>
> *Let them beat me! Little do they know of my luminous castles, my gardens bursting with flowers unparalleled anywhere, flowers that know how to sing and dance with love. In that distant land I am surrounded by butterflies, wise and golden butterflies coming to perch on the tips of my fingers.*
>
> Let them beat me! Little do they know . . .
>
> It was bitter cold, though, and he was shivering wildly.
>
> In my dream I cried all night, and when the orphan with those blue eyes—the deep blue of eternity—rose to depart, I suddenly thought I recognized him:
>
> Dear Child, my soul! (*HT* 7)

At least three aspects of this prose poem distinguish it as a remarkable piece of literature resulting from the genocide. First, while we cannot read it as other than a poem written by a genocide survivor, it never specifically refers to the Armenian Genocide but renders it *figuratively*, or *archetypally*. By doing so, Shēms avoids isolating the event as an historical anomaly and invites the reader to consider its meaning outside the specific history of Armenia and Turkey. Second, in the figure of the child here, Shēms objectifies (rather than merely recounts) his own exile as a survivor. That is, by portraying the orphan as an other, he not only creates a paradigm of the survivor who, beyond the horror and pain of losing his own family to violence, suffers the further humiliation of being himself ostracized in the diaspora (where he is "mocked" and beaten with sticks), but he also creates another voice, namely, the poem's speaker, the one who "crie[s] all night." This speaker expresses sympathy for the destitute orphan yet, at first, does not understand why. Shēms withholds, until the poem's closing line, the union of these two figures when the speaker suddenly recognizes in the orphan (at the moment of the child's departure, no less) his own soul. In short, he vividly dramatizes the double identity of the genocide survivor, depicting the rupture between self and soul brought about by such extreme violence.

Beyond these two dimensions of the poem, however, what is most compelling in "Orphan," once we begin to grasp its simply stated yet complex portrayal of the trauma of survival, is its utter lack of acrimony. To be sure, the poet has abruptly lost his family, home, community, past, and nation, yet in the poem only the weather is "bitter" and the night "bitter cold." Rather than submit to this bitterness himself, Shēms's frostbitten orphan innocently recounts his dreams and insists that "that distant land" with its "golden butterflies" is all that really matters. In "Orphan," in a few sobering lines, Shēms expresses the profound nature of the destitution yet shamelessness, the humiliation yet refusal to despair, that uniquely characterize so many of the survivors of the Armenian Genocide or, for that matter, of any other twentieth-century genocide.

The fact that Shēms did not compose "Orphan" until nearly a quarter of a century after the genocide is testimony to the very rupture it depicts. Yet Shēms knew all along that the only means of combating the evil that had befallen him was by releasing his poetic voice. He knew only too well that in order to gain back his life he somehow had to unchain that voice. In all modesty, he knew that in him dwelt his ancestors' bardic voice. He knew well that especially at times of national tragedy people long for poets to articulate and commemorate their anguish and fears. Deep in himself, he knew that his was such a voice, a voice strong and resonant enough to express the overwhelming grief of his people and a renewed hope for the future. Finally, he knew well that by breaking the shackles that had long muted his voice he might not only allay the pain and anguish of his people, but also quell his own suffering and realize his life's purpose. In a letter written to Gēvorgian on 19 December 1923, Shēms bares his soul:

There is a caravan of uncultivated themes in my soul, whose stay there brings only torture, yet I cannot invoke them; my fingers are bright red and I can barely hold a pen. The waves keep swelling without foam, without erupting. . . . It is time for us to say our Amen, no matter that light does not break through, that the sun and stars do not appear. It is our duty to say what we must. Why care about the result?[37]

As difficult and painful as this transformation was to be, the alternative would have been unthinkable—a falling back into the abyss of nothingness, into nihilism. And so, on a happy day, and against all odds, his powerful desire to survive broke his spirit free. The once darkened sun shone bright again, making 1923 a landmark year in his life.

By the end of that year, Shēms had some of his poetry finally published in two periodicals simultaneously: *Navasard* (Bucharest, Romania) and *Hrazdan* (Varna, Bulgaria). In an editorial note to the poems that appeared in *Navasard*, H. Ch. Siruni writes:

Those who have had the opportunity to begin a literary review know the feeling of dread that one reluctantly experiences upon seeing the pile of papers accumulate on one's desk on a daily basis. . . . Yet what a pleasure it is sometimes to find little gems among those stacks of papers, signed by an unknown, unheard name. You get the feeling that they have been enclosed in an unassuming letter by the quivering fingers of a shy young writer. And you experience the bliss of someone who has discovered a treasure, a new world, as well as something akin to pride, when you are persuaded to introduce to others this newcomer, who opens at first glance the budding flower of his soul.[38]

A few years later, reviewing the diasporan literary scene of the 1920s, Siruni characterizes Shēms's poetry as "a voice from the deep."[39] If the Armenian word "khorunk," meaning "deep," is translated into English as "the deep," it adds to its general meaning the image of the sea or the ocean, a connotation that seems to be so appropriate given Shēms's own love for the sea, both literally and figuratively. Another interpretation of the word "khorunk" would be "de profundis," the Latin term meaning "out of the depths of sorrow or despair," perhaps an even more appropriate reading. Still a third meaning forces itself on us: the voice that echoes from the past, the ancestral voice.

Though himself a Western Armenian, Shēms composed his early poems in the Eastern Armenian idiom. He was at home with both idioms. "Well-versed in both branches of Armenian literature," writes Mkhit'arian, "he nevertheless felt closer in language, style, and aesthetics to Eastern Armenian writers." While some of those poems echo the dejection and hopelessness he experienced, others spark a hope for a new life. In any event, because he was now actively writing and publishing, he had entered a cathartic period, a period that allowed him somewhat to alleviate his spiritual turmoil.

One of Shēms's most notable poems of this period is an ode to the poet, marked by an unexpected sense of joy, jubilation, at the thought of the unique power of the poet. Having gone where man can go no further, to the brink of nihilism, Shēms here attempts to rise above the fray. And images of the poet, larger than life itself, file through his consciousness as he offers this testament to the poet's inherent genius for shaping the world around him:

To the Poet

> Hey, poet! don't complain about your fate—
> Your soul, a darkened sky bejeweled with stars,
> Your heart, deep as the sea, yet more tempestuous,
> Your time all time, in the blink of the cosmos.
>
> With a tattered dervish's cloak draping your shoulders,
> You tread, under your feet, the crowns of the Caesars;
> And the blooming bough you bear forth like a spear
> Subdues the whole world, subject to your soul.
>
> You build the thrones where azure gods repose,
> Their shimmering blood colors your sword;
> Yet slaying gods, while still creating new ones,
> You're god himself, tatters draping your shoulders. (ĔE 85)

At the core of the poem is the enshrined and enthroned poet, "that hapless, tattered nobleman" who, despite (or maybe because of) his meager existence, now stands tall and unabashed. Indeed, he finds himself in the company of the gods, with his "time all time, in the blink of the cosmos," and upon reflection, he asks whether the gods themselves are not, in fact, nothing more than the creation of the poet's own imagination. Yet without arrogance, re-invoking the image of the tattered cloak draping the poet's shoulders, he maintains seeing the poet in the presence of the divine.

Throughout his life, Shēms published primarily under the pen name of Hmayeak Shēms [H. Shēms]. He was better known to the public, and even to his close friends and members of the family, by his pen name rather than his family name. Mkhit'arian correctly observes when he asks, "Yet who was in fact this man, this poet who, according to his passport, was actually called Hmayeak Sap'rich'ian—a name I believe he, along with the authorities or possibly even others before them, had virtually forgotten?" We do not know the circumstances that led Shēms to choose his pen name. Those who have broken bread with him, including the co-author of this text, his nephew, Vahé, never raised the question. He had always been Shēms to family and friends, *shāms* in Arabic, meaning "sun."

Today, we may wonder what led him to that choice? We can only speculate. Was it due to some deep-seated psychological reaction to his childhood basement apartment, "where the sun never shone?" Or was his choice related to some other poetic impulse, an unyielding love of nature perhaps, or pagan worship? Did it relate to a sense of mission he had wanted for himself? Or did it have more to do with aesthetics? Surely, he had given thought to the matter. For all we know, his reason may have involved any one or several of these considerations at once.

A second pen name Shēms later used was the Armenianized version of Shēms, namely, Aregents', in which case he signed *Aregents' H*. Besides these two pen names, he chose to sign one prose poem, entitled "O Heavens, How I Hate You!" as Hector Alani, published in the February 1945 issue of *Houssaper* [Husaber] *Monthly*. He also used other pen names for reviews and correspondence, such as H. Baret or simply H.

Shēms's given name, Hmayeak, too, has a fascinating resonance to the Armenian ear. It means "talisman," an object that often carries a magical power. In primitive thought, the name of a person is regarded as more than a mere appellation, but also an essential element of being, such as one's voice or shadow. The magical power inherent in the name Hmayeak connotes the potential to impel what is beneficial or salutary. And indeed, over time, Shēms successfully drew readers, near and far, to his poetry.

In the final analysis, for whatever reason(s) Shēms had chosen his pen name, that very act of choosing clearly demonstrates his drive to reinvent himself in the wake of the eradication of all he had known prior to the genocide. It also strikes at once a chord for the poet's own soul and for the Armenian diaspora for whom he was called to speak.

II

Poet, Scholar, Orator, and Teacher: Alexandria

MAKING SENSE OF HIS NEW ENVIRONMENT

In the summer of 1924, at the age of twenty-eight, exactly the mid-point of his abbreviated life, Shēms arrived in Egypt, weary from his endless wanderings. That same year, his younger sister Haykuhi, who had miraculously survived the genocide and taken refuge in Egypt a year earlier, had married Surēn Baladouni (born in Giresun, Turkey, some sixty miles [112 km] west of Trabzon on the Black Sea), also a survivor of the genocide. The couple had established domicile in the city of Zagazig, Egypt, and gave birth to a son, Vahé.

In Zagazig, Shēms was reunited with his sister whom he had last seen some fourteen years earlier on that memorable summer visit home in Trabzon. During the genocide, Haykuhi, together with other Armenian girls, had for a time enjoyed the protection of the city's Greek Metropolis. But the Turkish authorities soon ordered the Metropolis to release the girls. In an interview, remembering those horrid days, Haykuhi had just this to say: "My God! My God! What were we not subjected to!"[1] Though she lived to an old age (into her nineties), at no time was she able to talk openly about her experiences of the genocide.

From 1921 to 1923, Haykuhi lived in Greece where, despite her modest education, her innate teaching ability had enabled her to secure a position in an Armenian orphanage. There, among her students was Marie Atmachian [Atmadjian] (1913-) who later became known as a poet. In the early 1950s, Atmachian, upon the publication of her first volume of poetry, began corresponding with Haykuhi's son, Vahé, who at the time was serving on the editorial board of *Tchahagir* [Jahakir] *Weekly* (Cairo).

On that occasion, when she learned that Vahé was the son of her one-time teacher, she hastened to express her joy, saying: "Yes, dear Mr Baladouni, I know your mother very well for she, more than anyone else, has been able to leave an unforgettable impression on me because of her simplicity, intelligence, and artistic personality. From the period of my childhood in Greece, three things have deeply impressed me: the Temple of Apollo in Corinth, the sunny beaches of Loutraki, and my teacher, Miss Haykuhi."[2]

Vahé's father, Surēn,[3] who had Armenianized his Turkish sounding family name from Séraïdarian (*sarāy* meaning palace in Turkish and Arabic) to Baladouni, was at the time of the genocide a student at Perperian [Berberian] School in Constantinople. During World War I, he was drafted into the Turkish Army, but later, by his wits, he managed to escape and eventually found his way, via Aleppo, Syria, to the city of Zagazig, Egypt, where at the time there was a well-organized Armenian community. There he worked in the offices of an Armenian-owned cigarette manufacturing firm, Gamsaragan [Kamsarakan] Tobacco Company. Surēn's mother, Paytsar [Baydzar],[4] who had lost her husband, Dr Mihran Séraïdarian,[5] to the earliest round of Turkish atrocities, was forcibly deported, together with her mother and four children. Over the next few weeks, the unending desert road took the lives of Paytsar's mother and four children, and she had to bury each of them, one by one, in the forbidding, desolate lands with her own hands. At one point, crazed by pain and fear, she threw herself into the Euphrates River, but somehow she survived, living in the guise of a Turkish woman until Armistice Day, 11 November 1918. Following the Armistice, she began to search for her only surviving son, Surēn, whom she eventually located in Aleppo, Syria, from where they moved to Zagazig, Egypt, a short time later. But as fate would have it, after a few years, in 1929, she would lose him once again, this time to cancer. From there on, until her relatively early death in September of 1939, she devoted herself to Vahé's upbringing.

In 1924, with his sister's family now in nearby Zagazig, Shēms temporarily resided in Cairo. During his stay in Cairo that summer he came to meet Gurgēn Mkhit'arian and Hakob Oshakan, two well-known literary critics. In his "A Portrait of Hmayeak Shēms," written in 1952, Mkhit'arian relates his first memorable meeting with Shēms:

> I first encountered Shēms in a Cairo café one Sunday over twenty-five years ago. Our first conversation, held in the company of Oshakan, concerned the works of Eghishē Ch'arents'. Pulling from his pocket a slim volume printed in Moscow, in a deep and passionate voice Shēms began to recite from Ch'arents''s verse. Because he had known Ch'arents', he then told a few anecdotes, interjecting spirited comments of high praise. In fact, it later turned out that hearing those poems on that Sunday afternoon shaped Oshakan's own first impressions of Ch'arents'.[6]

A meditative Shēms. Alexandria, Egypt, 1924.

He then notes, "Immediately we were drawn to this rare and charismatic fellow," and adds:

> Shēms possessed a wealth of memories from the many cities he had visited and lived in, especially recollections of all the writers, political activists and books he had come across. And he harbored strong opinions about each of them, whether expressed with a profuse, hearty affirmation or qualified by a deep, fervent disdain. A truly original thinker, he was always highly critical, restless of mind and independent in his views.[7]

For the upcoming academic year, 1924-1925, Shēms was invited to teach at the Poghosian [Boghosian] National School of Alexandria. When he arrived in Alexandria, all traces of what was once the greatest city of the ancient world were gone.[8] Alexandria, and Egypt as a whole, was now entering a new era. The brief French occupation of Egypt (1798-1805) was followed by the rise of a new ruling dynasty. In 1805, an Ottoman soldier by the name of Mohammed Ali seized control of the country and established a dynasty, his successors ruling as khedives (the title used for Turkish viceroys in Egypt) and later as kings. In 1882, during a local uprising, which led to the killing of numerous foreigners, the British occupied the country and kept it under their sway until the end of World War II, though in 1936, an Anglo-Egyptian Treaty had given Egypt some degree of autonomy. During Shēms's years in Egypt, King Fuad was on the throne (1922-1936), succeeded by his son, King Faruk (1936-1952).[9] On 26 July 1952, shortly after Shēms's death, King Faruk was deposed in the revolution led by Colonel Gamal Abdel Nasser.

The rapid growth of Alexandria in the modern period (nineteenth to mid-twentieth century) owed itself primarily to the commercial energy of its cosmopolitan population—Greek, Italian, Jewish, and Armenian, among others. If during this period the Greeks played a major role in commerce and the Italians as architects and engineers, the relatively small community of Armenians, aside from their role in the country's commercial life, produced some of its most distinguished ministers: Nupar [Nubar] Pasha, Prime Minister; Tigran [Dikran] Pasha, Minister of Foreign Affairs; and Yacup [Yacub] Pasha Artin, Minister of Education, as well as other high-ranking functionaries. In his two-volume work, entitled *Modern Egypt*, Evelyn Baring (Earl of Cromer) notes: ". . . I may say that those few Armenians with whom I have been brought in contact appear to me to constitute, with the Syrians, the intellectual cream of the Near East."[10] During this era, the Armenian community in Egypt grew to become one of the major cultural centers in the diaspora.[11]

It was in this most Europeanized Arab city that Shēms lived the second half of his life. At Poghosian National School he was assigned courses in

Faculty of Poghosian National School with graduates. Seated, left to right: Instructor in Arabic, H. Amirian, Hmayeak Shēms, Nikol Aghbalian, Gabriel T'agvorian, M. Papazian. Standing: the graduates. Alexandria, Egypt, 1925.

Armenian language, mathematics, Armenian history, and ethics. The Poghosian School prided itself for having a congenial and progressive faculty. The principal of the school, Nikol Aghbalian, a noted intellectual and scholar, had served as minister of education and culture in the government of the short-lived Republic of Armenia, 1918-1920. H. Amirian, a one time colleague of Shēms, remembers fondly those early years when, at the end of the day, Shēms, Aghbalian, and he, among others, would spend long hours at a seaside café discussing educational, literary, and national issues.[12]

In those days, the overriding national issue was the Community's stance toward Soviet rule in Armenia. The very brutal Stalinist regime had split the Armenian diaspora into two antagonistic camps. On the one side was the Armenian Revolutionary Federation (popularly known as the Dashnak Party) with its fiercely nationalist-irredentist posture and, on the other, the conservative Armenian Democratic Liberal Party (popularly known as the Ramkavar Party), the Social Democratic Hnch'akian Party (popularly known as the Hnch'ak Party), and the relatively small pro-Communist Armenian Progressive Party. The Ramkavar and Hnch'ak parties' attitude toward the Soviet regime was a tactical one. They regarded Soviet rule in Armenia as a beneficial step toward ensuring ultimate independence, while at the same time enjoying Soviet protection against numerically and militarily superior Turkish forces. These major political lines kept the Armenian community of Alexandria, as elsewhere, bitterly divided, often sacrificing the national good to party interests. Unfortunately, one area that regularly fell victim to partisan politics was education.

The Poghosian National School where Shēms was employed is still located on an expansive property owned by the Armenian community. The grounds accommodate the diocesan offices, a church, an apartment building, a theater [Melk'onian Hall], an athletic field, beautiful gardens, and much more. On the grounds of this property, adjacent to the church, stands the elegant mausoleum of Armenian-born Nupar [Noubar] Pasha (1825-1899), a statesman who served as Egypt's prime minister for many years. The official address of this Armenian-owned property is 12 Sharia Baidawi (*sharia* meaning street), though it is more popularly known by the name of the main street on which the very extensive apartment building stands, Sharia Abou Dardar. Shēms taught at this community school for three years (1924-1927), at the end of which the conservative Ramkavar Party, having assumed power after the diocesan elections, dismissed all of the Dashnak faculty, including the principal, Aghbalian, and Shēms, much to the detriment of the community's educational system.

His insecure teaching career, on the one hand, and the horrid memories of the recent past, on the other, continued to keep Shēms in a state of agitation. In a letter dated 16 October 1924, addressed to Gēvorgian, he deplores how fast the days have gone by without his leaving a notable trace behind. The loss of the homeland continued to weigh heavily on him:

> . . . I feel that living so far away from our native soil greatly diminishes our drive and emotions. I cannot live my life now through the homeland, nor can I as a citizen of the world. The long night sits upon me oppressively; I seek a way out, a way of liberating myself. I wonder what you are doing as a wandering poet yourself, or what you are thinking. Do you have a prescription for melting, vaporizing, evaporating this iron wall of darkness?[13]

Yet, and despite the gloom that enveloped his soul, Shēms's early years in Alexandria were not unrewarding. With the collaboration of two of his colleagues—Gabriel T'agvorian and Benyamin T'ashian—Shēms undertook the publication of a pedagogical review, *Hay Varzharan* [Armenian School], printed in Cairo by *Houssaper* [Husaber] Press. In the ten issues that were published from March to December 1926, Shēms signed a number of articles, such as "The School and Character," "Abnormal Children in School," "Psychoanalysis," "The Education of the Will," and a series of articles entitled "Azgayin dastiarakut'iwn" [National Education]. This last series focuses on the critical role Armenian culture and tradition plays in the formation and education of Armenian children in the diaspora. Shēms held as self-evident that while there are marked similarities among the earth's peoples, significant differences have also evolved over time, giving rise to the varied groupings known as nations. These long-standing differences account for the often-conflicting ways in which nations view, comprehend, and judge world affairs. Although it did not exist at the time Shēms was writing, the presence of the United Nations in our own time testifies to the reality of the circumstances Shēms observed.

With reference to this periodical, to which he also contributed, Gēvorgian writes: "This undertaking to which Shēms devoted himself stood as the best of its kind in the post–World War I period. It attracted the work of prominent educators such as Levon Shant', Nikol Aghbalian, A. Astvatsaturian, and H. T. Hintlian." In association with the journal, pedagogical seminars were held at the Poghosian National School on the works of A. Fouillée, Jean Piaget, William James, and others.

During those years, Shēms also contributed to such publications as *Nor Sharzhum* (Cairo, Egypt), *Hairenik* [Hayrenik'] *Monthly* (Boston, Massachusetts), and *Houssaper* [Husaber] *Daily* (Cairo, Egypt). V. Srvandztiants', a well-known Armenian composer, set to music some of Shēms's early poems [Paris, 1926, 1927].[14] Now not only was Shēms's reputation as a poet widening, but also the inherent lyricism of his work and its deep reflection on the Armenian soul were beginning to attract the attention of other artists and thinkers.

FLIGHT TO PARIS

Because of the continuing instability of his teaching career, Shēms, with financial assistance from a close circle of friends, left Alexandria for Paris in the summer of 1927 to study psychotherapy. There he enrolled in courses at the Fondation Henri Durville and other institutes, obtaining appropriate professional diplomas. Henri Durville,[15] writer and psychotherapist, founder of the International Psychical Society and editor of *Journal Du Magnétisme*, on more than one occasion expressed his admiration at Shēms's successful experiments in magnetism, remarking: "I am not surprised; after all, you are a product of the East, are you not?" implying, of course, the existence of some mystical powers inherent in healers of the East. Impressed by Shēms's performances, Durville later invited him to join the faculty of the Institute. However, there is no evidence that he did. Among his personal papers, there remains a visiting card, which reads: Professeur H. Shēms (Médication psycho-naturiste), 12 Rue des Ecoles, Paris Ve, Tel.: Gobelins 27-58. This may suggest that Shēms practiced psychotherapy privately while in Paris, or he may have intended to, but nothing else substantiates that he actually did. What we know is that during his two-year stay in Paris, Shēms contributed articles to *Buzhank'*, an Armenian-language medical journal.[16]

A search of Shēms's archive does not reveal any noteworthy remembrances of his years in Paris. Instead, his more direct impressions of the city are found in a letter written from Paris to Gēvorgian:

> Paris did not cause me to marvel at it; it is a city and nothing more. It is said that it is necessary to live here a long time in order to savor its charm and beauty. So be it! Beauty and kisses flow on the sidewalks; however, what fascinates me is theosophy. Paris is perhaps the only place that gluts one's senses with external impressions, such that man is driven to introspection in pursuit of the spirit. He must search for himself in a sea of tens of thousands, his frail poetic soul murmuring like Verlaine, "Sad is the flesh."[17]

Commenting on Shēms's letter, Gēvorgian writes:

> His artistic soul has an explanation for every phenomenon and image. He who knows the best figures of the French school of poetry suddenly inscribes the words or name of one or the other onto his own canvas in order to strengthen the appeal of and add grace to the point he wishes to emphasize.

Indeed, only one poem, the prose poem entitled "Meghavor kinĕ" [That Sinful Woman], written some fifteen years after his return from Paris, takes as its subject a location in Paris. In this poem, Shēms finds a telling affinity between the suffering of those in the Armenian diaspora and that of others throughout the world who seek solace in the figure of Mary Magdalene.

The poem recounts how one oppressive autumn day, while wandering the streets of Paris, a welcome downpour of rain finds the poet taking shelter in the Church of St Magdalene. There, seated in a pew, his eyes rest on the high altar. And he is alarmed at what meets his gaze:

> In an Armenian church I would find there the image of the Holy Virgin Mary, the Mother of God, with the Infant Jesus pressed tightly to her breast. But here it is that sinful woman, Mary Magdalene. It is a marble statue that occupies the main altar, facing to the side and leaning slightly forward, her hair flowing abundantly over her face.

Struck by the stunning appearance of this beautiful, yet "sinful" woman, he later muses:

> This is the rare moment for meditation, introspection. The tiny lights stir in me ceaseless, eternal tears. Sitting in the shadows, I sense it is still raining . . . Oh, how many afflicted, anguished, agonizing hearts, seven-times wounded, are here! They [the nuns] have carried their stricken souls to this sinful woman who understands them so well, who can feel deeply their sleepless, undying sorrow. How fortunate that there are canonized sinners on this earth. What joy for humans that a God incarnate has lived with their tribulations, loved them, and forgiven them. (HT 39-43)

Despite being immersed in the cosmopolitan atmosphere of Paris—being removed not only from his birthplace but from his second home in Alexandria—as these lines attest, Shēms never shook off his anguish from the losses he and others incurred from the genocide. Here in this far-flung (for him) and worldly city, what does he discover that most deeply impresses his memory? Not its grand symbols of liberty, culture, and spirituality, but a quiet sanctuary for those who have survived terror. "What joy for humans," he concludes, "that a God incarnate has lived with their tribulations," so that they need not suffer them alone. In his creative life, it is this unexpected corner of Paris that means the most to the poet.

Indeed, deep in his soul, Shēms recognized that he was destined to share the life of his own people and to speak for them, to provide solace for them in his own way. While this sense of his Armenian identity reveals itself throughout his works, in none is it expressed so poignantly as in his prose poem, "Tesilk' T'orgoma Tan Hamar" [A Vision for the House of T'orgom] which we shall discuss in a later section, "The Passion that Chose Shēms."

MOMENT OF TRUTH

Shēms was still in Paris when word came of the death from cancer of his brother-in-law, Surēn Baladouni. Faced with this unexpected turn of events, Shēms, without the desire to start a family of his own, decided to return to Egypt to assume responsibility for his brother-in-law's family, including his brother-in-law's mother, Paytsar, his now widowed sister, Haykuhi, and her four-year-old son, Vahé. Shēms departed Paris, and his sister moved with her son and mother-in-law from Zagazig to Alexandria, where together they took up residence at 11 Rue Abel, Ibrahimiya, a subdivision of a suburb known as Ramleh (meaning *sands* in Arabic). The suburb extended from Silsileh, a low-lying promontory to the east of the graceful Eastern Harbor, to Montazah, some seven miles (12 km) farther east, where the royal family had its summer residence. Along this seafront drive, known as the *corniche* (the French equivalent for "drive" along a coast), lie many beaches: Chatby, Ibrahimiya, Sporting, Cleopatra, Stanley Bay, San Stefano, Sidi Bishr, Miami, and Mandarah, among others. In the easterly half of the *corniche*, there were also at the time many beautiful villas with extensive gardens.

In the subdivision where Shēms lived, the housing pattern was rather mixed. There were a few villas of the very rich, but it was mostly comprised of apartment buildings serving people of varied economic strata. Vahé remembers well the modest attic apartment where the four of them lived, atop a two-story house surrounded by several mulberry trees, some shrubbery, giant sunflowers, a grapevine, and hosts of colorful flowers. Unlike Shēms's boyhood basement apartment where the sun never shone, here in this attic apartment the sun rushed in from every window and door. However, the roof leaked in half a dozen different places during heavy rainfall and pots and pans had to be placed strategically under the drippings.

The first and second floor apartments had four bedrooms, but the attic apartment had only two; the remaining area constituted a large open portico or veranda, as it was called. Surrounded with plants, it was an ideal place to relax in a chaise longue or comfortable armchair (though Shēms never did), while Vahé played his imaginative games on the floor; otherwise, the streets of the neighborhood served as his playground. Of the two bedrooms, the larger one accommodated Paytsar, Haykuhi, and Vahé, the smaller one Shēms and his belongings, consisting of his bed, books, and manuscripts. Shēms wrote primarily on lined, legal-sized paper, folded lengthwise like the width of a newspaper column; sometimes he also used the backs of envelopes, and the inside of cigarette boxes and book matches. A makeshift bookcase, somewhat buckled under the weight of its contents, leaned against the wall at one end of the room. Other books, along with manuscripts, lay scattered on a nearby table and across a couple of chairs. On one of the chairs, amidst the books and papers, glittered his pocket watch. A few ashtrays, containing the butts of the poet's Italian black cigars and burnt incense, were found around the room. He usually hung his clothes on a hook behind the door.

Family reunion. Seated, left to right: Shêms, Paytsar, Surên. Standing: Haikuhi with Vahé. Zagazig, Egypt, 1928.

A third room, into which one stepped from the landing of the outdoor staircase, served as a living room, dining room, study room, and guest room. On one of the walls of this general purpose room was a portable oil lamp. Across from it, on the opposite wall, was a map of Armenia. This map was not just a single map, though, but four maps in one. It showed the boundaries of the Armenian SSR, the 1918-1920 Republic of Armenia, historic Armenia and, finally, the boundaries of Armenia as drawn by the American president, Woodrow Wilson (1913-1921), for ratification by the signatories of the Treaty of Sèvres (10 August 1920). The Wilsonian borders, which awarded some 16,216 sq mi (42,000 sq km) of the eastern Ottoman provinces to the then existing Armenian state, never materialized. The remaining wall space carried family pictures, including those of the many relatives who had fallen victim to the Turkish atrocities. The general scarcity of living space was, however, more than compensated for by the love in the family. During the summer, they even welcomed relatives and friends from Cairo to spend their vacation with them.

In downtown Alexandria, Shēms opened a clinic where from the start he had great success vocationally. In this connection, Gēvorgian writes: "I had heard of his successes in his [new found] profession from Nikol Aghbalian and Levon Shant'." Writing to Gēvorgian around this time, Shēms speaks of his intention to earn some money and move to India, apparently to embrace the ascetic life:

> I am glad to hear that Nikol [Aghbalian] has told you some things about the miracles I am performing . . . Egypt is an open field for these cures; I hope to make a little bit of money and then go to India. I have transformed the poetry of the page and the book into this kind of poetry or, if you will, this kind of madness, as some would say. The great Armenian nation has not given the world such madmen, whereas other nations have contributed many. It is a shame to our great nation; in order to wipe this stain off, I am ready to go mad, to lose myself on the road toward the unreachable.[18]

Whether Shēms is being serious or intentionally ironic in this revealing letter, he later had to discard his plan to become an ascetic or a monk. His destiny lay elsewhere. He knew only too well that, no matter where he wandered, his Armenian ethnicity would inevitably follow him, and that sooner or later he would have to return to his true spiritual roots and the soil that had nurtured it, namely, Armenian literature and culture. Anyway, his practice did not last long. While vocationally successful, financially it was a disaster due to his inability to run it on a sound business basis. He was too generous toward his clients. A year later he was forced to abandon his practice.

Indeed, fate, in which Shēms believed, had ordained him to return to the classroom. But as the governance of the Armenian community was still in the hands of anti-Dashnak parties, he could not return to his former teaching position. Faced with this situation, he spent the next five years (1930-1935) as a visiting professor of Armenian language, literature, and history at two local private schools—Haykaznian Gymnasium and the Palayan School—giving at the same time private lessons to Armenian students attending foreign schools. He continued to contribute articles, reviews, and poems to *Houssaper* [Husaber] *Daily*. Also, in the 1933 issues of *Hay Dprots'* [Armenian School], a pedagogical review published by the Armenian Teachers' Union in Egypt, he signed several articles, such as "The School and the Home," "Imagination and Moral Education," and "Let Us Respect the Children."

"[While] rich in dreams," writes Mkhit'arian, "[Shēms was] yet meager in his ability simply to deal with everyday life." As a breadwinner, he could hardly keep himself and his adopted family afloat. In 1932, in hopes of turning things around, Shēms applied for the position of principal at Melk'onian Educational Institute in Nicosia, Cyprus. But as the School was already in negotiation with another candidate, Shēms withdrew his candidacy. The continuing deterioration of the family's financial situation had already forced Haykuhi by 1930 to seek work outside the home. Fortunately, a suitable job was found as she assumed the position of director at the *Armenian Girls' Home* in 1930, an institution run by the Armenian General Benevolent Union (AGBU). She occupied this post until 1935.

In 1935 the *Home* closed its doors for lack of residents. In her autobiography, the one-time chairperson of the *Home*'s Board of Trustees and a well-known writer in the community, Victoria Arsharuni, pays tribute to Haykuhi, describing her as "a young widow from a good family, intelligent, and graceful, who was able to inspire love and respect in us all."[19] After the closure of the *Armenian Girls' Home*, Haykuhi devoted her time to caring for her mother-in-law, until she died just before the outbreak of World War II.

Shēms had embarked on a teaching career at the tender age of seventeen and continued to teach for the rest of his life, with the exception of his two-year stay in Paris and the year he practiced psychotherapy in Alexandria. After the 1935 diocesan elections, when the Dashnak Party carried the day, Shēms was invited to return to Poghosian National School, a teaching position that was financially more rewarding than his combined teaching posts at the Haykaznian and Palayan schools. Nonetheless, given the rising cost of living, his financial situation hardly improved. In the same undated and unfinished letter addressed to his childhood friend and classmate Arshakuni, Shēms writes, "On the occasion of the latest elections, when our side emerged victorious, I was rehired, and I remained in that post through the difficult war years during which, unfortunately, the high cost of living inflicted more damage on us than the daily enemy attacks."[20]

In 1938, in the middle of these difficult times for his family, Shēms had the pleasant surprise of seeing, if only for a brief moment and from a distance, his older schoolmate Gēvorgian, with whom he had last met some fifteen years earlier at a seaside café in Constantsa, Romania. Gēvorgian, who had at one point moved his family to Beirut, Lebanon, had next taken the "adventurous step," as he calls it, to relocate himself and his family to Buenos Aires, Argentina. As the boat on which they were traveling, *Le Mariette Pacha*, cast anchor at the Alexandria harbor, Gēvorgian, through a local messenger, sent word to Shēms and another friend to come to the port. Upon their arrival at the wharf, the two men made visual contact with Gēvorgian who, from the balcony of the boat, introduced his wife and children to them. But all they could really do was to exchange silent looks of longing and friendship and wave *adieu*, as the three-chimney ocean liner finally lifted anchor and headed toward the open seas.[21]

More than just financially, Shēms's life continued to be one of ongoing struggles. In a letter to Gēvorgian, dated 17 August 1938, he lays bare his agitated soul once again: "I am not guilty for my delinquencies, for my life is a tumultuous one. I may, perhaps, best express myself by these two lines from Isahakian: 'My day is dreary, nothing but black; / my hope rests on the morrow.'" Throughout the letter, Shēms's love of his homeland still continues to consume him:

> It is so onerous to live away from one's homeland. I would rather that materially my life be a thousandfold worse, if only I could be in my own land, next to my kith and kin, among my people . . . My soul has an insatiable thirst for those of the same ilk and for a more compassionate world.
>
> I can smell the odor of death throughout the diaspora. My soul writhes powerlessly and in despair. Out of my pain, I emit screeches of hope, but all the while the truth that devours my soul plunges me into a deadly darkness. These are my death pangs . . . but I keep trying to wrestle them.[22]

From confessions such as this, it is clear that, despite his love for his sister's family, his earnest devotion to his teaching, and his accomplished writings, he could still not shake off the specter of the genocide that continued to haunt him.

Nevertheless, Shēms persevered, driven by the love of his work and never losing faith in his vision of an eventual return to a reborn Armenia. During his nephew's childhood, on the occasion of King Fuad's, and later, King Faruk's birthday, as a special treat, Shēms would take the younger Vahé to the *corniche* where spectacular fireworks marked the happy event. At the end of the celebration, Shēms would turn to Vahé and say: "The day will come! The day will come when we shall witness our very own national celebrations in our very own homeland." Shēms did not live to see that day, but Vahé has.

TWO PUBLICATIONS: *ṚOSHNAKAN* AND *SAYAT'-NOVA*

Despite the demons plaguing him, Shēms was able to find contentment in his adopted community of Alexandria, where he produced the far greater portion of his works. Some writers see scores of their works published during their lifetime, others as few as a single volume. In his own lifetime, Shēms saw the publication of two books under his name: *Ṛoshnakan* and *Sayat'-Nova*. The first, *Ṛoshnakan* [Luminous], published in 1943, contains a collection of his poetry and prose writings. The second, *Sayat'-Nova: Matean imastut'ean, geghets'kut'ean ew anmatuyts' siroy* [Sayat-Nova: Book of Wisdom, Beauty, and Unrequited Love]—a study of the life and works of the renowned eighteenth-century Armenian bard (*ashugh* in Armenian)—appeared the following year. Both works were published in Alexandria by A. Step'anian Press, and authored under his pen name, H. Shēms, followed by Aregents' H. in parentheses. He owed their publication to the sponsorship of friends. Still, despite their modest beginnings, these two books, along with others, published some five decades after his death, secure for Shēms an important place in Armenian literature.

The title of his first book, *Ṛoshnakan*, a rarely used word, is the adjectival form of the noun *ṛoshnut'iwn*, meaning luminosity. Of the various connotations of the word, such as *luminous*, *open-hearted*, *candid*, and *sincere*, Shēms's intended meaning was "luminous," although one can make a case for the meaning of any one of them or all taken together. Whenever the question arose during his literary gatherings with colleagues and students, Shēms did not fail to emphasize his intended meaning: *luminous*. He had a fascination with light-giving sources, be they celestial, intellectual, or spiritual. His very pen name, meaning "sun," underscores this attachment. His writings inevitably look toward this luminosity, to shed light on the darkest corners of the human soul.

Ṛoshnakan is divided into two parts, essays and poetry. In a later section, "Serving the Word and Poetry," we discuss Shēms the poet and his poetry. Here, in broad outline, we shall characterize his prose. The essays further divide into two groups: those that address universal themes and those with a specifically Armenian focus. A good portion of his prose takes essay form: observations and reflections on human culture. The essays with universal themes tend to exalt an ideologically healthy civilization while at the same time pointing out the aberrations and symptoms of unjust and ailing social orders. In "Mardkut'iwnn u ir tagnapĕ" [Humanity and Its Crisis], he underscores the sacredness of life, which no power should be able to suppress, let alone take away. "Living," he notes, "should be a right, not an ability," if we are to put an end to the universal crisis. (*Ṛ* 35) In "Vripats k'aghak'akrtutiwn mĕ" [An Aborted Civilization], he deplores the extent to which humankind has bound itself to material life: "Despite its spiritual struggles, humankind has remained heavily attached to the material world. Physical comfort and bodily pleasures have become its trophies of victory." (R 42) And in "Mer zhamanaknerē" [Our Times], he deems civilization to be an illusion, and worse, the foundation of hypocrisy. Civilization is meant to elevate the individual morally, intellectually, and spiritually; instead, it has turned out to be nothing more than "an embellishment of human instincts." Later, he notes: "Without being bedazzled by the glitter of human artifacts, we can unhesitatingly say that humanity has denuded itself, stripped itself of all its frocks. Not even a fig-leaf now covers its nakedness for there is neither shame, nor shamelessness." (R 45) Shēms debates these rather grave and weighty topics in a graphic and telling language.

Equally noteworthy are his essays on Armenian themes. They pay tribute to the Armenian genius, the Armenian people and its history, but they often take a rebellious stance against the destiny imposed upon them. Shēms venerates everything Armenian: life, people, country, history. In an essay entitled "Pētk' ē shach'ē . . ." [Let It Resound!], he writes: "Armenian life is a magnificent and glorious temple, and its ascent an ecstasy, the primary truth and beauty of the universe." (R 111) Other essays on themes such as the Armenian home, mother, school, teacher, elite class, and youth are critical expositions meant to engender love for Armenian culture and to keep Armenian communities in the diaspora linked to national ideals. Indeed, in an essay, entitled "Hay ĕntranin" [The Armenian Elite], he lays down the mission of the diasporan leadership: "It is our task to link the present to the future; yet everything in the present comes from *yesterday*. Our social environment must be filled with the vitality of the *past* centuries so that our decisions and hard work of today be fruitfully linked to the *morrow*." (R 158) These essays, like those with universal themes, are rich in lofty thoughts and oracular utterances.

Shēms's second book, *Sayat'-Nova*, is a study of this renowned eighteenth-century minstrel's Armenian songs (Nova wrote in three Caucasian languages: Armenian, Georgian, and Azerbaijani). It includes sixty of Nova's Armenian songs with lexical annotations; the musical score of eight of the most popular songs; a rich glossary of more than a thousand words and phrases (indispensable for understanding Nova's dialect); and a rendition of twenty of Nova's best known songs into Western Armenian which, to a remarkable degree, retain the sense, the rhythm, and the flavor of the original. Shēms introduces the volume with an innovative study of Nova's life and works.

Noted for their outstanding improvisation, subtle lyricism, and wisdom, Nova's songs gained him a reputation as a first-class minstrel. This reputation, in turn, secured him a position at the royal court of Irakli II of Georgia, where he lived until his banishment in 1759, presumably due to his opposition to the aristocracy. In a poetry permeated with love and harmony,

Nova considers love as the eternal source of earthly life, with human life ranked supreme. In his analysis of Nova's poetry, Shēms observes: "Nova's high-spirited life stories are matched only by a language which adorns and animates his songs with colorful, vivid imagery." (*SN* 17) In an astute comparison of Sayat-Nova to Omar Khayyám, he notes: "The Armenian bard does not suffer the Persian poet's anguish of vanity for he does not lack in purpose; he knows how to lead a dignified life on earth and, from its *narrow window*, to aspire to eternity." (*SN* 18) Shēms also senses in Nova's lovesongs "the gentle aroma of Armenian love, a love that can unhesitatingly be deemed singular in the world." (*SN* 29) Finally, he underscores Nova's awareness of his own genius, as well as his deep regard for human emotions and the allure of art itself.

Regarding this work, some sixty years after its publication, Henrik Bakhch'inian, a Sayat-Nova scholar himself, writes: "To this day [Shēms's study] maintains its freshness and value."[23] In tribute, Bakhch'inian republished Shēms's study of Nova's life and works as well as his rendition of Nova's twenty most popular songs into Western Armenian in his edition of Nova's complete works (*Khagher: Liakatar Zhoghovatsu*, 2003),[24] dedicating the volume to Shēms's memory.

CHASHKA CHAÏ: AROUND A CUP OF TEA

Since his initial arrival in Alexandria in 1924, Shēms had been active in the local chapter of the *Hamazgayin Educational and Cultural Society*. His numerous lectures and speeches gave life and depth to that Society's programs. Aside from this involvement, he also became an active supporter of the Alishan Cultural Association, founded by his Armenian Catholic students. He contributed to its development as a group and, over the course of several years, gave edifying lectures before its membership. Aside from these activities, he gave public speeches on such special occasions as the celebration of the Invention of the Armenian Alphabet[25] and Armenian Independence Day (28 May 1918).

However, during the early years of World War II, as a result of the frequent bombings of Alexandria, the cultural activities of *Hamazgayin* ceased. Unlike Cairo, which was declared an open city and therefore entitled under international law to immunity against bombardment, Alexandria was a target for air raids. In September 1940, Italian troops crossed the border from Libya and advanced some sixty miles into Egypt, and by the early months of 1942 the Axis forces under the command of a young German general, Erwin Rommel, nicknamed "The Desert Fox" for the skillful military campaigns he waged, came perilously close to Alexandria. It was not until November of that year that their advance was finally checked by the

Allies at El-Alamein, some sixty miles west of Alexandria, from where they were ultimately forced to retreat before year's end.

During those two years, the city was blacked out after dark and placed under a curfew. Air raid warnings sounded nearly every night, followed by the assaults of Italian and German aircraft that drove residents into municipal shelters, as well as the basements of high-rise apartment buildings converted into shelters. During the air raids Haykuhi and Vahé would take cover in a nearby shelter, but Shēms, despite his family's desperate entreaties, refused to abandon his attic room. During one air raid, a bomb exploded in the vicinity of their residence causing the windowpanes of their attic apartment to shatter. It was a close call for Shēms; still, he never budged from his decision to remain in his attic room no matter how severe the attacks.

Once the North African War subsided, Alexandria could resume its normal life and the cultural activities of *Hamazgayin* were revived. At that time, a group of young men joined together under Shēms's leadership and guidance, to dedicate themselves to restoring the literary-cultural life of the community. They held literary forums on the works of Armenian writers, past and present, including a special presentation of the life and songs of Sayat-Nova. On stage they presented such plays as Molière's *Le mariage forcé*, Shakespeare's *The Merchant of Venice* and *Othello*, Shirvanzadē's *Patvi Hamar* [For One's Honor], and Levon Shant"s *Inkats berdi ishkhanuhin* [The Princess of the Fallen Fortress] and *Kaysrĕ* [The Emperor]. Even later, when Shēms, due to his failing health, could not participate regularly in the meetings of the Committee, the group continued to be led by his inspiration and advice.

Passionately devoted to *Hamazgayin*, Shēms bestowed his faith in, and adoration of, Armenian culture as a legacy to his young friends and admirers. In his memoir, Perch Momchian, a writer, editor, and disciple of Shēms, recollects those times:

> We believed firmly that it was culture, and culture alone, that could replace the absence of our native land, creating a spiritual homeland. And we sought occasions for celebrating Armenian culture. To implement our plans, we would naturally turn for advice to the one who had venerated Armenian culture in his own right so fervently. That person was none other than Shēms.

Momchian then goes on to describe the gatherings of the group, which were held at least once, and often twice, a week:

> We knew where and when we could find Shēms. At nightfall, we could find him at Khach'ik's grocery store, located at the entrance of the Armenian populated suburb of Ibrahimiya [on Rue Pelouse]. There he would be savoring the appetizers Khach'ik prepared.

Occasionally, we, too, enjoyed Khach'ik's sandwiches, especially the one he prepared with scrambled eggs and cured beef [*apukht* in Armenian].

He then gives us a glimpse of the atmosphere of the meetings:

> We did not tarry long at the grocery store. Led by our master, we would move to *Oasis*, a corner coffeehouse, where we would order tea or soft drinks, finishing up our sandwiches and continuing our informal discussions late into the night.
>
> We would have an outside table reserved for us. During those open-air meetings, the Italian black cigars that Shēms smoked never bothered us. Indeed, so engrossed were we in our exchange of ideas that only occasionally would we look up to notice the alluring young girls passing by.[26]

These meetings came to be known as *Chashka Chaï* (*Чашка Чай*, Russian for "cup of tea"), named after those gatherings that used to take place at Hovhannes T'umanian's attic apartment in Tiflis, Georgia, at the beginning of the century. The group that gathered there had included well-known poets, writers, and scholars, such as Ghazaros Aghayan, Levon Shant', Nikol Aghbalian, Avetik' Isahakian, Derenik Temirchian and T'umanian himself. Modest though the Alexandria group was compared to the Tiflis group, it was equally devoted to the cultivation of Armenian culture.

While Shēms had his regular followers, on occasion that number doubled with the participation of friends of the group. Sometimes, when the meetings were held at Shēms's attic apartment, Vahé, too, would participate in them, while Haykuhi was only too happy to serve the group the traditional *chaï*, as well as to contribute to the ongoing discussions. Within a broad spectrum of literary and artistic issues, recollects Vahé, the group discussed the works of Armenian and French writers and poets, such as, on the Armenian side, Gregory of Narek, Sayat-Nova, and Khach'atur Abovian, and on the French side, Stéphane Mallarmé, Charles Baudelaire, Paul Verlaine, and Paul Valéry.

To be sure, these readings and discussions also had their light moments. Now and then, when the exchange of ideas would heat up, Shēms was quick to interject humor into the conversation. He was witty and jocular. As a poet, he was just as at odds with modern obscurant poets—the futurists, for example, who often presented an incoherent and anarchic blend of words stripped of their meaning and used for their sound effect alone—as he was with the Parnassians who emphasized the objective, the impersonal, the impeccable form to the exclusion of the ineffable intuitions and impressions of the inner life. There were also times when aspiring writers in the group would read from their own writings. As Shēms used to say whenever matters of creativity were raised, "There is nothing new under the sun; what is new lies within you."

REPATRIATION: *DEPI ERKIR* [HOMEWARD BOUND!]

Following World War II, word came out that there would be repatriation to Soviet Armenia. With the blessings of the Soviet government, the Armenians of the diaspora were permitted to emigrate to their homeland. The move was enthusiastically embraced by the Armenian Church throughout the world as well as the Ramkavar and Hnch'ak political parties. Sadly to say, the Dashnak attitude toward the repatriation (*nergaght'* in Armenian) was at best cool. For Shēms, it was a hopeful sign of yet better things to come. Early on Shēms had championed repatriation, keeping the love of the homeland burning in the hearts and minds of the multitudes. In 1936, he had made a heartfelt call for repatriation, "Depi erkir" [Homeward Bound!]. His call was unambiguous: "Let there be death there! Let us die there! For death in the homeland is the mother of new, eternal lives, while Armenian existence in exile is nothing but a barren, prolonged and painful death." (ĚE 341-343) And when, in the spring of 1948, the doors of repatriation were finally flung open, he was among the first to welcome it whole-heartedly. At the same time, he was saddened to see his own party maintain at best a hands-off policy in response to this historic event.

No sooner was the repatriation officially launched than Shēms began to speak to his students in support of it. The higher echelons of his party reprimanded him for doing so, but he ignored them. Before long he was invited to address a mass meeting organized for promoting the repatriation. Again, the party's governing council opposed his participation, this time issuing him a stern warning. And once again Shēms paid no heed. "[Shēms] never tolerated a party policy that did not make sense to him," writes Step'an Shahpaz. He then observes:

> Nor did he ever deny his party affiliation, nor his biases, very much like a man of faith; even there he maintained his integrity. . . . He always maintained an independent stance vis-à-vis the party elite, showing disdain toward any policies dictated from the top tier. He would never betray his own principles.

> In Shēms the sense of pride had an Armenian muscle. But this was not born out of conceit nor a *complexe de supériorité*. To the contrary, it emerged from the keen sensitivities of the true intellectual, a truly human being. From this perspective, he never yielded.

Reflecting on Shēms's speech at the historic mass meeting, Shahpaz writes:

Armenians may boast of many patriots among themselves. In this respect, too, the standards are relative. But Shēms's patriotism was one of his most fundamental and unyielding characteristics. Only once did I hear him speak in public on the subject, during a mass meeting held to promote Armenian repatriation from abroad to the homeland. His speech dwarfed the most ardent of speeches or writing by others on the subject. He said what no one had dared say or could say. Therein resounded the quintessence of patriotism; and he expressed himself freely, without restraint, subject only to the cries of his heart.[27]

Nevertheless, once he dared to defy his party's will, he was shunned by them for the rest of his life. Furthermore, his party's long arm reached as far as the critic Oshakan who, under pressure, reluctantly omitted Shēms's poems from his anthology of Western Armenian literature. Yet through all this Shēms remained unshaken. He dismissed his party's retribution as petty vengeance. This undeniable wrong, which at the time was echoed in the Armenian press,[28] was not really set right until more than half a century later with the publication of his works by Baikar Association in 1994, and later by the Eghishē Ch'arents' Museum of Literature and Art in Erevan, Armenia, 2001- 2004.

SERVING THE WORD AND POETRY

In Armenian literary circles, there is general consensus that Shēms has played many roles. Of the many, we single out here only four: *teacher, orator, scholar, and poet*. Mkhit'arian sees the roles Shēms played as parts of a single whole, all radiating from the same spiritual source: "It is, in short, unnecessary to label Shēms as either orator, poet, journalist, teacher, scholar or political activist. Quite simply, he was all these things, with none overshadowing the others, but all integral, inspired, genuine, unique and dynamic."

As a *teacher*, Shēms was at once loved and revered. Even idolized. One student, speaking for the many, writes: "The entire class worshipped him."[29] And another notes in gratitude: "He shared his knowledge, his wisdom, with us all, for little or no compensation. This man, weary and exhausted, when he interpreted the lessons of history, of Armenian history, would suddenly unfold himself like an eagle, with a glow of national pride sparkling in his eyes, talking all the while in a resonant voice, full of enthusiasm."[30] In his turn, Archpriest Haykazun Voskerich'ian, principal and owner of Haykaznian Gymnasium, has this to say: "Shēms had noteworthy qualifications. He had character, talent, education, erudition, and competence. As a teacher, he possessed a mastery of each subject he taught; he was ebullient and inspiring. The students loved him and his classes."[31]

Literary critic Gurgēn Mkhit'arian (right) with Shēms. Alexandria, Egypt, early 1940s.

But Shēms was not merely a classroom teacher. He was a teacher in the style of a *Zarathustra* or Kahlil Gibran's *The Prophet*. When he spoke, he engaged his audiences' whole psyche, rather than just their intellect. Progressively educated and shaped by the circumstances of his own life, he had gathered much wisdom, which he readily and lavishly shared with those around him. Mkhit'arian ably portrays Shēms, the teacher and his message:

> A natural teacher, Shēms could often be found on the steps of a school or in a classroom, where he spoke to students enthusiastically about the beauties of the Armenian language and its literature, or of Armenian history—the glorious achievements of "the Armenian race." He lectured and taught everywhere, inside and outside classrooms, on streets or in cafés, on stages or in churchyards, even in homes, like one of Socrates' disciples, always surrounded by both his old and his new students who were mesmerized by him, students who would maintain their association with, and respect for, him even after becoming parents themselves.

Not only as a teacher, but as an *orator*, Shēms, this "hapless, tattered nobleman," aroused deep feelings of national pride and identity in the hearts and minds of his audiences. Yet he was never the narrow-minded ideologue; he never failed to criticize shortcomings where he saw them. Mkhit'arian underscores this point when he writes: "Still himself even on stage, Shēms was adept at thrilling his audiences with the power of his ideas and the passion of his convictions, as he attacked all public indecencies, injustices, and illegalities, turning each into an object of derision." Momchian, in his turn, captures Shēms, the orator, with this image: "An erudite speaker, he was the jewel of our stage. When he spoke, the audiences overlooked his somewhat shabby looks. His soul-stirring gaze gave him the aura of a modern-day prophet. And, indeed, many of his prophecies [such as the rebirth of the Republic of Armenia in 1991] came to pass."[32]

Alongside the teacher and orator stood Shēms the *scholar*. Far removed from the rich literary resources of his homeland and equipped only with his own learning, a precious few scholarly books, and his poetic intuition, Shēms toiled tirelessly in the vast field of Armenian history, culture, language, and literature. He firmly believed that literature occupies a critical place in the life of a nation. "Every nation has its soul," he wrote. "Every nation expresses its soul through all the imaginative arts—indeed, through all those things, which the hands touch and over which the mind labors. But chiefly, it is through literature that a nation's soul finds its clearest expression." (*PHG* 23)

In the years 1941 and 1942, Shēms delivered a major lecture series on Armenian literature to alumni and upper-class students of Haykaznian Gymnasium. They encompassed the history of Armenian literature from its oral traditions in antiquity up to the early years of the twentieth century.

The lectures covering the ancient and medieval periods were simultaneously published in serial form in *Houssaper* [Husaber] *Daily*. Those relating to the modern period (from 1800 on) remained unpublished due to World War II shortages of newsprint. Sadly, the lecture notes on the modern period have been irrevocably lost. Some sixty years later, in 2002, the Eghishē Ch'arents' Museum of Literature and Art in Erevan, Armenia, republished the surviving pages under the editorship of Henrik Bakhch'inian, complete with endnotes and a lexicon of nearly six hundred words. In his scholarly introduction to the volume, Bakhch'inian welcomes this work as "the first complete history of ancient and medieval literature published in the diaspora." He then praises Shēms's astute observations on and characterizations of many of the past figures and events. Finally, he notes that while Shēms considered these lectures a "modest work," they are to be regarded as nothing less than a "feat," a *tour de force*, "especially given the trying circumstances under which they were prepared and delivered." (*PHG* 6-7)

Following the lecture series of 1941-1942, Shēms wrote an essay on a theme that may arguably challenge critics of Armenian literature. Entitled, "Mets azg erek' mateanov--urvagits" [Great Nation with Just Three Books: An Outline], Shēms boldly asks: "What is the measure by which it would be possible to evaluate the greatness of a nation?" Finding the criteria of numerical count and sheer intellectual power inadequate, he proposes the criterion of *vogeghinats'um*, a propensity toward spiritualization, and argues that a nation's supreme expression of greatness lies in the spiritual content of its literary works. (*ĒE* 325) From among Armenian literary figures, he selects the works of three—Sayat-Nova (1712-1795), Khach'atur Abovian (1809-1848), and Gregory of Narek (951-1003)—as epitomizing the supreme spiritual expression of *love, nation, and God*, respectively.

"On the gentle strings of Nova's *kemancha*"[33] Shēms sees "the transformation of the crude, animalistic sexual instinct into boundless sacrifice, the renunciation of the narrow self for the yearning of the sweetness of the immaterial, incorporeal life." (*ĒE* 326) In Abovian's *Wounds of Armenia* he sees "an expression of selflessness, a tempestuous immersion in the life of the collectivity." "The entire nation is present there," he writes, "right in Khach'atur's wounded heart, and he is one with his nation, with its pains and future." (*ĒE* 326) And, finally, in Narek's *Book of Lamentations* Shēms sees "the luminous revelation of the crises and the ultimate state of spiritualization of the Armenian soul." He notes that "[Narek] is boundlessly fired up with eternity" and "the miraculous transformation of the earthly man into divinity." (*ĒE* 326)

Having viewed Shēms the teacher, orator, and scholar, we can, finally, and perhaps most significantly, turn to Shēms the *poet*. As we know now, Shēms's early poetic voice was abruptly muted by the onset of the Armenian Genocide of 1915. For some eight years sorrow and anguish fiercely dominated his being, clinging to him like vipers, threatening to extinguish his voice permanently. To reiterate his own words, "There is a caravan of uncultivated themes in my soul, whose stay there brings only torture, yet I cannot invoke them. . . . The waves keep swelling without foam, without erupting." Yet those seemingly barren years actually served as years of germination, a period during which a more mature poetic voice was forged in his subconscious. The polish came over time. In 1923, Shēms's voice finally burst through taking him from his debilitating isolation into creativity and lyricism.

Gēvorgian, an admirer of Shēms's works, writes this of his poetry: "Most of Shēms's poems are written in a highly symbolist language, condensed and clear. An intense music rises from the very heart of his poetry, expanding the allure of compressed beauties."[34] The use of the word "symbolist" in Gēvorgian's critique need not necessarily suggest that, in any strict sense, Shēms adhered to the French Symbolist school of poetry. To be sure, he had no urge to belong to any particular literary school. Rather, by generating images that work as metaphors or embody emotions, he articulates his intuitions, the sensual impressions of his inner life. The vivid imagery, taken with the poems' deep, sonorous music, confers on Shēms's poetry a psychic vigor so intense that it has led Mkhit'arian and T'agvorian[35], among others, to label Shēms's poetics as *vogeghinats'um*, meaning with "a propensity toward spiritualization," a term Shēms himself uses as a critical criterion for gauging literature. This poetics, emphasizing spirituality and exaltation but without becoming doctrinaire, is best phrased by Mkhit'arian as "the Poetry of Pure Spirit."

Shēms's mature poetry (1923-1951) may be roughly divided into three thematic groups: *Armēnakan*, *Sirayin*, and *Tervishakan*. The first of these, *Armēnakan*, meaning *unique to Armēns or Armenians*, contains those poems that bear on Armenian identity; the second, *Sirayin*, literally meaning *of love*, refers to his love-songs and romantic poetry; and the third, *Tervishakan*, meaning *in the manner or style of a dervish*, includes his philosophical poems.

Armēnakan, the first of these categories, includes poems that bear on momentous national events, such as the Armenian Genocide of 1915 (commemorated on 24 April) and the Independence Day of the short-lived Armenian Republic of 1918-1920 (celebrated on 28 May), as well as poems that generally and unequivocally glorify the Armenian genius, culture, and history. An example is "Im Nayiri" [My Nayiri], a bold, lyrical poem that venerates the abiding Armenian spirit. In order to emphasize the constancy and longevity of that spirit, Shēms invokes the ancient appellation "Nayiri," the name used to refer to the land and people of Armenia during the late Bronze Age:[36]

> To my burning spirit, yearning, you are a poem, my Nayiri,
> You, for ages, a mere plaything in the hands of the mighty, my Nayiri,

> You, who amid the turmoil of the East embody its salt and savor, my Nayiri,
> You, who gleam with the dawn's sacred promise, my Nayiri.
>
> My Nayiri, you so lofty the world has never reached nor captured you,
> Your soul prevails, pure and impervious, as both victim and penitent,
> And never have you faltered, never wavered, even in fleeting light,
> You, the unyielding beam of justice of the true masters, my Nayiri . . .
>
> Countless conquerors come and go; yet here you stand, still known;
> The more they blackened your sun, the brighter and greener you became,
> Your spirit, like your mountains, enduring, blooming, indomitable;
> Eternally reborn, you are the fiery elixir of life itself, my Nayiri . . . (ĚE 47)

Set in a mythic context and timeless present, as though being spoken across centuries, the poem extols the perseverance of the Armenian people who, despite multiple invasions and the untold devastation of their land, have somehow endured, transforming their trials into triumph through literature, architecture, and music. In a tone somber yet hopeful, aggrieved yet exalting, Shēms celebrates Armenia's complex history, especially its unfettered determination to recreate itself. While the poem incorporates conventional symbols from nature—light, mountains, the sun, "blooming" landscapes, and so on—Shēms invests each with a kind of alchemical power to portray not only Armenian history but the "fiery elixir" that has kept that history alive into the present.

Another poem, entitled "Armenakan salin vra" ([The Anvil] ĚE 54), likens the endurance of the Armenian people to an anvil fixed in eternity. The strident tone of the poem strikes a balance with the mighty poundings of the ruthless conquerors, turning, in the last verse, into the reverberations of the anvil's song of victory. In bold strokes, Shēms brings into relief the historical image of a people who, despite the innumerable adversities, have maintained their resiliency and remained on the world's stage, while their one-time conquerors have vanished from existence. Implicit in the poem is a very simple yet powerful message directed to would-be conquerors.

Shēms's love-poems, *Sirayin*, constitute a second category. It includes his idealized utterances of a universal human emotion so characteristic of poets. A number of these songs portray romance and heartbreak. Among his lovelorn poems, one entitled "Kinĕ" [La Donna] (ĚE 71), compares a man's need for a woman's love to the whitecaps of the ocean to which a desperate, drowning person clings in order to save his life. Yet, deep in his soul, Shēms recognizes the powerhouse that true love can be. In the poem "Yar Asatsd" [True Love], he sings of the virtues of true love:

> May love be like a freshly ripened fruit.
> May love be like a book of meditations

Sought out in time of crisis—brilliant, pure.
May love be like the refuge of oblivion.

May love remain forever blind to strangers.
May love be like the soul's most precious sisters,
Or like a gentle violet, sweet and fragrant,
May love remain both kind and unpretentious.

May love shine like a bright star through the dark.
May love endure like hope, untouched, untainted,
Like sunlight cast across death's black abyss,
May love rise ever like the breaking dawn. (ĒE 73)

In a slightly bardic (*ashughakan* in Armenian) voice, as though echoing a poet from an earlier age, Shēms celebrates the potential virtues of the love between a man and a woman in a series of similes that range from the worldly to the cosmic. Composed as a litany of energetic, sinewy sentences woven into each other, the poem achieves its effects through the sheer accumulation of detail. After comparing love's physical beauty to a "freshly ripened fruit," Shēms defines love's virtues, one line at a time, in concrete as well as abstract terms—considering it "sweet and fragrant" as a violet, on the one hand, yet "unpretentious," on the other, yet by the end, "like sunlight" able to be "cast across death's black abyss." This alignment of extremes in defining love recalls, among other influences on Shēms, his early interest in Nietzschean thought. Nevertheless, the delicacy in sound and sense of each line individually conveys the tenderness of love without resorting only to conventional figures to depict it.

In his last love poem, "Kazel" ([*ghazal* in Persian, meaning ode] ĒE 82), written in 1948, Shēms takes on the Persian poetic form of the *ghazal* as his model, but he does not strictly adhere to it. He observes the rule of repeating the last word in each couplet in the first and fourth couplets, but not in the second and third. In this beautiful piece he reveals the love he has held most dear throughout his life: the love for his own love, the love for his own God. His *ghazal* cascades with graceful solemnity and an inimitable charm and ease.

Tervishakan, a third category of Shēms's poetry, collects his philosophical musings on a variety of themes. In a good number of these poems, he takes on "life" itself as a theme, personifying it as seductive lass who clings to us tightly and makes us her humble, obedient servants. Other poems treat impending death, often composed in the *andante* of a funeral march. A relatively long, seven-part poem, entitled "I khorots' srtits'" [De Profundis], develops a meditative discourse with God. In it Shēms challenges God to descend from his eternally azure paradise to be instilled with the blood of the poet so that "His soulless heart begins to fathom the great pain, the great sorrow of the human heart." (ĒE 93-97)

A few musings are about him. One such poem is "Ark'a" [Monarch] in which he reveals his compassionate self:

> No king known—not one!—draped in purple robes
> Has, with his proud cortege, his own realm graced
> As I have this one, roving majestically
> Through its strange, foreign streets, bright, open-faced.
>
> I stretch my hand to each of countless brethren,
> Even to those who balk or turn away,
> And under each foot cheerfully I spread
> My heart's imperial colors on display.
>
> I mix my boundless mirth with others' glee,
> My clanging cymbals freely on all bestowed,
> As through my soul's tears, clear as sunlit rain,
> I eagerly hand out my joy, like gold.
>
> In tattered rags, how mightily I stroll
> With my own entourage, stately and grand,
> Through foreign streets, as no king has strode before,
> Nor ever will go forth through his own land. (ĒE 117)

In this celebratory and, in its broadest sense, deeply spiritual poem, Shēms expresses his own humanity. With unquenchable vitality voiced in passionate language, the speaker portrays himself "roving majestically" through city streets and immersing himself in the pain of all those he encounters, perhaps to alleviate their suffering or perhaps just to convey his affinity with them, as he "cheerfully" spreads his "heart's imperial colors" beneath their feet. Yet the vivid image here of a "bright, open-faced" monarch proudly clanging his cymbals for all he passes is balanced by the equally vivid, and by-now familiar image throughout Shēms's work of the exile in "tattered rags"—dislocated, starving, and alone—wandering "strange, foreign streets." Nevertheless, as the poem's strong rhythms and energetic phrases emphasize, the speaker finds his own happiness almost exclusively in the happiness of others. And indeed, given this credo, despite his lifelong émigré existence, Shēms considered himself a kind of Croesus.

In whatever category a Shēms poem may fit or whatever form it may take, each bears his unmistakable timbre and unique style: a propensity toward spiritualization. Nevertheless, this dominant characteristic of his voice he plays out with a spontaneity, simplicity, and luminosity that belie its solemn nature. Moreover, the speaker in a Shēms poem comes to embody not merely the individual, nor even a particular psychological identity, but a whole people's character. Still it is this abiding poetic trait, this propensity toward spiritualization, that distinguishes him most from other Armenian poets of the post-genocide generation.

In addition to his poems and essays, Shēms has composed a number of fables, such as "Paths to the Summit" (*ĔE* 129), an eagle's encounter with a worm on the lofty summit of a mountain; "The Discontent of the Camels" (*ĔE* 132-133), the camels' complaint that the donkey has been chosen to lead the caravan; and "The Pig Victorious" (*ĔE* 130-131), the pig's challenge to the lion-king as to who truly is the monarch of the forest. These fables work as allegories that further reinforce Shēms's cultural and spiritual themes.

He has also penned some fifty quatrains, all of which convey his broad and compassionate world-view (*ĔE* 137-146). Mention must further be made of his very successful translations from Charles Baudelaire, Paul Verlaine, Théophile Gautier, Feodor Tutchev, Aleksandr Pushkin, and Friedrich Nietzsche, among others (*ĔE* 157-164).

THE PASSION THAT CHOSE SHĒMS

To appreciate fully the depth as well as the complexity of the passion that chose Shēms, we must bear in mind two momentous events he experienced in his lifetime. First, as made evident by the course of his own wanderings throughout his adult life, was the Armenian Genocide of 1915, which inflicted deep wounds on Shēms's soul—wounds that would never heal. This great pain, one that millions of Armenians would come to share with him before the twentieth century would run its course, cast him into physical as well as spiritual exile. For Shēms, perhaps the most profound effect of the genocide was not only its direct impact on those who died and their loved ones who happened to survive, but the way it has come to shape the generations of Armenians born long after the actual massacre itself. He understood the danger of a catastrophic history that predates yet permeates an entire people. The second was the impending threat of assimilation, which also took its inevitable toll on Shēms. As waves of Armenian refugees flowed from the historic lands of Armenia into the Middle East, Europe, and the Americas, the encroaching fear of yet another kind of genocide, known as *assimilation* or *white massacre*, began to creep into his heart, as it did into the hearts and minds of newly formed Armenian communities everywhere. Gēvorgian underscores the latter point when he writes: "Shēms deeply understood the dangers facing the diaspora. Even today, few are those who feel them as deeply as he did. Shēms lived out the tragedy of those impending threats."[37]

Engulfed by both the dark memories of the past and the gloomy prospects for the future, Shēms had to seek a way out. To try not to think about them, to try to keep them at bay or out of his consciousness, if at all possible, would have required enormous amounts of psychic energy. In the face of such unrelenting anguish and fears, and short of a nihilistic rejection of life, how could he rise to the challenge? Put another way, how could he overcome his suffering, the flood of grief, which had estranged him, alienated him from life itself? Fortunately, Shēms himself provides us with an answer, found in two prose poems, both written in 1939, nearly a quarter century after the genocide. In the first of these, entitled "Alien," he raises the question of alienation:

> I realize, still I realize, these are my hands. My feet obey me. Why, then, this estrangement? In familiar streets, in plain view, old acquaintances gaze at me in astonishment. Even in my own house I find I am a stranger. Why don't they recognize me? Am I not one of them? I call out to myself. I summon me . . .

And in summoning himself, he finds to his horror

> an old empty tomb, lying in ruin. Not even an echo. Alas, something besides silence, something more than loneliness, has fallen here, allowing even the hollow cold to shudder." (HT 9)

The very simplicity of Shēms's diction and imagery creates an immediacy of feeling, an intuitive sense of the soul's predicament. It is almost as though he has uncovered a layer of self-annihilation or a void in the self beneath the common experience of existential weariness. Yet he expresses this state of emptiness with an eloquence and stark beauty that virtually belies the speaker's sense of grief.

Then a brotherly voice confides to him:

> Don't believe those are your hands. Don't believe that your feet obey you. Dear to us as you may be, you are nothing but a ghost, a mere trace of memory who mockingly reminds us how fragile even the base of monuments can be. We sense you like a flash of lightning on the horizon, a chance fragrance from afar.
>
> Yet, if you want us to acknowledge you, stop wandering aimlessly, stop smiling benignly like such a child. Get going! Strike your feet on the ground, firmly. We will recognize you by the sound of your steps. Start walking! We want to be able to hear you.
>
> Start walking! We want to know who you are. (HT 9, 11)

By dramatizing here the exchange between the alien and his own conscience, Shēms succinctly portrays the estrangement that an émigré, a person torn apart from himself, experiences. This prose poem also expresses the guilt, as well as the obligation to continue living, felt by those who have survived a catastrophic event from which so many others have perished.

Indeed, this poem anticipates comparable works composed by survivors of the Nazi Holocaust and those who lived through the bombing of Hiroshima, not to mention later occurrences of mass killing. Yet this very complex psychic state Shēms presents with the clarity even a child could understand.

In a second prose poem, entitled "The Ghost of T'orgom,"[38] the poem's speaker is in utter despair: "Cast onto foreign streets far from home, deeply distressed, I felt abandoned by all I knew, but by none more than by myself. Drawn into the abyss of despair from which no one returns, in my soul I plunged over and over again into the vast, dark wild . . ." It was then, at that moment of black chaos, that he hears the voice of ancestral wisdom echoing gently in his ear: "Arise! Armēns never die merely for the sake of dying. They die artfully and for all eternity. . . . And suddenly, in that same moment, I could feel the pounding of the ages under my feet. I knew I was not just one Armēn with the ability to die. Eternity stirred in my slumbering veins." And he wonders:

> Was I in a trance? Was I asleep? Maybe it was a dream. But as a single Armēn I no longer seemed to exist. Century after century after century in all their poignant majesty kept parading before my eyes and through my soul. And the future—times not yet come, times I could hardly have envisioned before in my meager everyday life—invaded my being with each grand beat of my heart, seeking the crash of the cymbals deep in its core.

Shēms is now face to face with the ghost of Armēns (a version of the name *Armenians*), that "eternal guardian of the House of T'orgom" (House of T'orgom refers to the Armenian homeland) who commands him to go out and do what he has been called upon to do: "Go to your brothers and sisters, old and young alike. Go to all of them, to every one of them, and thunder into their hearts the spirit of Armēns, so majestic and grand, soaring from the four corners of the earth to the sacred land of Ararat. . . ." And adds:

> I have molded your heart, your feeble heart, into a drum to proclaim what is yet to become of Armenians everywhere. Rise and stand tall like me. Go from door to door, as through your beating heart I rouse all who are despairing or dormant. Go now! Armēns are not fearful people. Do you believe they could have possibly traversed the forbidding mountains of the past in fear?

Strengthened by the voice of T'orgom, Shēms's own long-muted voice finally breaks loose, opens up, as his long-silenced heart lets forth its cry. He stands tall and starts alerting his fellow Armenians both inside and outside Soviet Armenia of the dangers of assimilation. Near the poem's close, he exhorts his people to "keep their ancestors' home alive" in the wake of its own potential annihilation:

> [Go] and proclaim to my people that I [the spirit of Armēns] live and so will they. I shall guide them through the world's storms and turmoil, but only if they, the undying, indomitable Armēns, keep their ancestors' home alive, speak in their own mellifluous language, and nourish themselves on their ancestors' food.

And in a final gesture, the ghost adds:

> Likewise, they must learn to embrace the virtues they experience in the lands of their wanderings, bring them back to their own homeland and nurture them there, and, most important, not stop believing that the present is always full of wisdom for those who seek it. The gods will die only when you do, no matter how much they want to live on as lovers of eternity. (*HT* 13, 15, 17)

Shēms's belief in Armenian culture is so strong, so unwavering, that despite the immense suffering he has both witnessed and experienced, he sees it enriched, not threatened, by the struggle for survival by those throughout the diaspora. Yet, in his eyes, this cultural enrichment can be meaningful only if it is brought back to the homeland and nurtured there. Herein lies Shēms's view of "cultural nationalism," his complex sense of patriotism.

In this unfolding drama, Shēms comes to the full realization of what he must have known all along in his spiritual unconscious: that he had a voice equal to the historic moment, a voice strong and deep enough to articulate not only the common sorrows and fears of his people, but also their determination to overcome the tragedy that had shrouded the entire nation. For more than three decades his distinctive voice was heard everywhere from classrooms to family homes, from cafés and the streets of Alexandria to lecture halls and open air mass meetings, from the pages of political newspapers to the pages of scholarly periodicals, and from literary gatherings to published tomes. The immeasurable sorrow and hardship he faced throughout his life, like that of most Armenians, was matched only by his will to reach some kind of reconciliation and by his very genius for doing so.

HIS WANING YEARS

Much has been said and written about Shēms's drinking habit. As in all cases of a perceived or real frailty in a public figure, Shēms's drinking, too, often became a point of contention. When he resigned from his teaching position at Poghosian National School in 1945, some attributed his resignation to his drinking habit. In fact, the record shows that Shēms had requested the school's Board to relieve him from full-time teaching responsibilities and reassign him as a visiting professor of Armenian studies so he might devote more time and energy to his creative work. Since school authorities were not agreeable to his request, holding that a teacher of Armenian subjects should be a full-time member of the faculty, Shēms decided to resign instead. His decision was somewhat helped by the fact that by now his nephew was gainfully employed and able to shoulder the household expenses. A couple of years later, he was offered a two-year contract (1947-1949) as principal at Khrimian National School in Kirkuk, Iraq, but he declined. He was reluctant to leave Alexandria, which by now had become a "home" for him. Then in 1949, he resumed a visiting appointment at the Haykaznian Gymansium, where he continued to lecture until the year before his death.

If, during this period, Shēms's literary productivity did not particularly increase nor did it decrease. Judging from his list of publications, Shēms continued to maintain his previous level of output until the end of 1950. Among other things, he wrote several short stories and some poetry. He was willing to do more, such as write plays,[39] and render Khach'atur Abovian's *Verk' Hayastani* into Western Armenian (see Appendix C), but his physical powers were not serving him as well as before. His drinking habit was beginning to show the ravages wrought on him.

In the first half of 1951, he could barely devote his energies to anything more demanding than refining and republishing some of his earlier translations from French and Russian poets, including Charles Baudelaire (1821-1867), Paul Verlaine (1844-1896), Félix Arvers (1806-1850), Théophile Gautier (1811-1872), Aleksandr Pushkin (1799-1837), Fyodor Tyutchev (1803-1873), and Dmitry Merezhkovsky (1865-1941). (*ĔE* 157-164) His translations of Baudelaire's "Au Lecteur," "Bénédiction," and "Recueillement" were published in *Akos* [Agos]: *Bimonthly Journal of Literature and Art* (Beirut: Issue No. 6, 1951). During this period Shēms also wrote one last poem, entitled "Armenian Requiem," commemorating the Armenian Genocide. It was published in the 24 April 1951 issue of *Houssaper* [Husaber] *Daily*. (*ĔE* 61)

By the second half of 1951, Shēms's health took a turn for the worse. During those difficult months, his devoted sister, Haykuhi, and equally devoted nephew, Vahé, provided him with the best care possible. Indeed, the emotional stress created by Shēms's failing health was more than compensated for by the abiding love of his sister and nephew. Because he suffered from insomnia, his nights were usually nightmarish, as Shēms preferred daylight and the gentle warmth of the sun. While his condition was a longstanding one, it had by now reached dangerous proportions. In one of his prose poems, entitled "Night," Shēms reflects on the torment that the dark often brought him:

> Claws planted deep into the horizon, jaws gaping toward the sky, Night—guardian of criminals, patron of lovers—stretches across the city like a huge monster.
>
> Night has invaded my heart and crushes it without mercy.

Yet night also brings with it the promise of a new day:

> Night also knows how to sing; it sings of Tomorrow with tenderness soft as velvet, and it sings of the Sun.
>
> Steadily, the darkness is pricked and pierced. O, it's so wonderful! Soon again it will be light. People will greet each other, and the Sun will stroll again across the sky, smiling on their twitches and wounds.

Then with a touch of irony, he continues:

> O, and how kind Morning can be.
>
> *Good day, my brothers!*
>
> Entwining each other, the vipers of evil submerge to the depths of the fading dark, and today, once again, there will be light.
>
> Today, too, we shall love each other, and today, too, we shall hate each other. Today, once again, we shall live, waiting and hoping once more, hoping patiently for the calm of Night, the rapturous music and shadowy intrigue of the darkness . . . (*HT* 25)

During this period, Shēms's concerned friends and colleagues frequently visited him in his attic apartment. To the end he cherished the fellowship of his former students, colleagues, and loyal disciples. On days when Shēms mustered enough strength, Vahé would take him to Nouzha Gardens where they enjoyed a tête-à-tête conversation at the picturesque Antoniades Café. On other occasions, a Greek taverna served as their meeting-place.

Quite apart from the friendly atmosphere Shēms enjoyed, there was also an antagonistic stance on the part of some, the so-called power brokers, toward him. As Shahpaz points out, "Shēms had both followers and enemies. It would be unlikely, indeed impossible, to believe that such a man of ideas, one given to expressing himself candidly and fearlessly, would have only friends, only sympathizers." He then notes:

And, of course, Shēms had his faults—human frailties—just as everyone does. Any other man of his temperament, ideas, sensitivity, would have easily succumbed to them. But those shortcomings harmed himself more than others, and sadly so. He drank; he poisoned himself a little each day. He may have had his reasons for it. Or maybe his drinking was an act of fate. A rebellion.[40]

Nearly a quarter of a century after Shēms's death, Surēn Kēonchian, a former member of the Armenian Diocesan Council (*K'aghak'akan Zhoghov*) of Alexandria, who looked at teachers, and in particular, at Shēms, with some animosity, for what he considered their excessive influence on younger minds, would write: "One fiendish night [Shēms's] body was found lying on a sidewalk. After a few days' stay at a hospital, he settled his affairs with this world."[41] Aside from this statement, for which there is no corroboration, Kēonchian also refers to Shēms's poem, "Burial," as a "last will and testament," written only days before his death. As we know, the poem in question was written not days, but some thirty years before his death and published in *Navasard* in 1923. Indeed, two months after the appearance of Kēonchian's article, Smbat Hokhikian, a well-respected member of the Armenian community of Alexandria, responded to Kēonchian's memoir with his own recollections. Published in the same newspaper, Hokhikian refutes Kēonchian's many baseless assertions, including the accusation of Shēms's public display of drunkenness.[42] On this score, Mkhit'arian cautions us from overplaying the effects of Shēms's drinking:

> Still, do not think of Shēms as a drunkard. To the contrary, he was a man who loved wine or ouzo in order to enjoy a few carefree moments, to remain above, so to speak, the mire of the world, the shabby affairs of mankind—and to share a toast or a table with those who were simple in spirit and noble in heart: the plain folk.[43]

Throughout January and February 1952, Shēms was completely confined to bed in his attic room in Alexandria and cared for by his devoted sister. By then Vahé had moved to Cairo on business. As Shēms's condition worsened, he was transferred to the Anglo-Swiss Hospital, located on a rise along what was then the Abuqir Road, where, at community expense, he received the best of care under the watch of an expert medical team for the entire month of March. Before long, the hospital became a pilgrimage site. Each day, during visiting hours, students, friends, party members, and disciples, young and old, surrounded him. In his last days he had become practically speechless. However, two or three days before his death, he suddenly sat up in his bed and, summoning all his strength, declared to those around him: "*The Armenian nation shall live! Shēmses come and go, but in the end our nation will triumph and live."* With these last words, almost said as his own epitaph, Shēms closed his eyes on the world.

EPILOGUE: HMAYEAK SHĒMS—THIS MAN, THIS POET

As we look back on the life and work of this rare, charismatic figure, we discern in him the presence of a truly compassionate human being endowed with a special spiritual gift: an original poetic voice. This unique voice, however, would not fully evolve and realize itself until the second half of his abbreviated life. After Shēms spent a certain amount of time groping and experimenting with writing poems in his younger days, the Turkish atrocities against its Armenian population—centering on the genocide of 1915—came to steal from him his youthful enthusiasm for life and planted in its place *"le vide, et le noir, et le nu"* [emptiness, blackness, and starkness], as Baudelaire would have said. For the next eight years or so (1915-1923) Shēms lived the deepest gloom of his life, wandering aimlessly from the Caucasus to the Balkans as a lonely, tormented soul. And though he eventually was able to transform his life from a near-nihilistic existence to a productive literary life, the habit of drinking he picked up during this period hounded him for the rest of his life.

Those seemingly barren years, however, were to turn out to be years of germination from which a mature poetic voice would blossom. The reaping was to come in good season, as Shēms finally emerged from his self-destructive isolation around 1923. In that year, he experienced a spiritual transformation: the despair that had long clung to him, threatening to silence his poetic voice permanently, began to dissipate slowly. In its stead, sparks of hope began to ignite his soul. The following year, still weary and exhausted from his wanderings, but strengthened by this new sense of purpose, Shēms landed in Alexandria where he lived (except for a two-year period of study in Paris) until his death. Though "a lone émigré in search of Mt Ararat and its shade," he found some solace in the Armenian community of this extraordinarily cosmopolitan city by the Mediterranean Sea. Here "he fought against life practically every day, every hour, without ever fearing death, always toiling, always creating, always serving the Word and Poetry." Though destined to "plow many new furrows in the literary domain" and "make us heirs of so many more literary gems," however, Shēms left behind relatively little work.

The paucity of his literary output may be attributed partly to his excessive drinking and partly to a severe case of arthritis from which he suffered during most of his adult life. As early as 1923, he wrote to Gēvorgian, saying: "There is a caravan of uncultivated themes in my soul whose stay there brings only torture, yet I cannot invoke them; my fingers are bright red and I can barely hold a pen." Over time this condition only worsened. Just a year before his death, in a letter to Geghard (pen name of Harut'iwn Gazanchian, 1928-2006), editor of *Akos*, he wrote:

> Geghard dear, please forgive me for delaying my response. I could not write because I was sick and still am—pains in my joints . . . pains in my joints . . . Under those circumstances, your note was a great comfort to me as I lay in lethe and oblivion, listening to symphonies of pain throughout my body.

Elsewhere in that letter he noted: "I have quite a large number of incomplete works."[44] Sadly, the incomplete works to which he refers, along with other archival materials in the possession of his nephew, Vahé Baladouni, perished in New Orleans from Hurricane Katrina in August 2005.

Nonetheless if Shēms's œuvre is quantitatively modest, qualitatively it represents nothing less than a paradigm of the Armenian soul. Like a pebble cast on the quiet waters of a pool, Shēms's work continues to generate new crests, as his posthumous publications attest. Future scholars of Armenian literature, investigating Shēms's works more thoroughly and more closely, may well reveal a contribution far richer than the number of the publications suggest. For example, one may cite how Shēms's language shows the way to reshape the long-standing differences between Eastern and Western Armenian literary idioms. As Bakhch'inian notes, "As a creative writer, Shēms's language is a most unique fusion of Eastern and Western Armenian literary idioms."[45] Another critic, Gēvorg K'rist'inian, also sees in Shēms's language a literary-cultural idiom that unites Eastern and Western Armenian both in terms of its form and of its usage. He observes further that Shēms's pan-Armenian mode of thought is "a phenomenon rather rare in our times."[46] Now that an Armenian nation has been restored, and given the large numbers of Armenians living in the diaspora, Shēms's attention to the division in the Armenian language is today even more relevant than it was during his own lifetime.

Shēms's image as "a wandering minstrel, a troubadour, who for all appearances wasn't from this world and who gave more to life than life had given to him," rings true to those who knew him in person. A great teacher, charismatic orator, tireless scholar, and poet of "pure spirit," Shēms's emotional and spiritual life is inextricably woven with the horrific events of his lifetime. The enormity of the Armenian Genocide, coupled with the fear of assimilation, continued to keep Shēms in a state of agitation until his death. Yet despite the ravages that life had inflicted on him, Shēms found the way to consider himself a Croesus.

Like the form and content of a beautiful poem, Shēms's life and works remain inseparable. Forged in the night of his spiritual unconscious,

Shēms's voice cascades like the clear, pure waters of a fountainhead. His various genres of works are full of wisdom, giving us keen insight into the human condition. His poetic voice radiates an aura of energy. Immediate yet luminous, melancholic yet filled with compassion, familiar yet unique, plainspoken yet sublime, his poetry touches the reader through the creative power of its imagery and inner music. In virtually every line, Shēms celebrates the primacy of the human spirit. And while his works are firmly rooted in his own era, they have lost none of their relevance and appeal for us today.

It is befitting here to raise the curtain on this rare and charismatic poet and man of letters one last time. A poet, first and foremost, whose voice was temporarily silenced by the horror of the Armenian Genocide, but then recovered, is here addressing the centuries that lie ahead. In his poem entitled "T'vank'" ("Seemings"), written in 1939, which we have retitled as "Statue," Shēms imagines his own place in times yet to come:

> Sometimes to myself I seem
> An ancient marble bust,
> My eyes recessed and dim,
> My deep voice hushed.
>
> I keep awaiting the age,
> With heads and hearts held high,
> When new lives filled with grace
> Will meander by . . .
>
> Look at these new people passing
> Who know not tears, nor disasters,
> Nor mercy, nor hope, nor blessing,
> Nor slaves and masters . . .
>
> Children, like roses, they sprout.
> They frolic in the sun,
> While my mad heart cries out
> Through this lifeless stone . . .
>
> To myself sometimes I seem
> An ancient marble bust,
> My eyes recessed and dim,
> My deep voice hushed. (ĚE 121)

Marked by a sense of tranquility, dignity and, above all, stirrings of a new life, the poet finds for himself a permanent place in an endlessly changing world. While the shock of his traumatic past lingers in the folds of his memory, yet through his poetry—with its language fixed in "lifeless stone" like that of a "marble bust"—he feels liberated, liberated from seen and unseen oppression. And he believes deep in his soul that his bardic voice will continue to resonate in the hearts and minds of future generations of readers. He knows well that he has secured a place for the things he loves in the ever-growing canon of Armenian literature.

Appendix A

A Portrait of Hmayeak Shēms

Gurgēn Mkhit'arian[1]

I first encountered Hmayeak Shēms in a Cairo café one Sunday over twenty-five years ago. Our first conversation, held in the company of Oshakan[2], concerned the works of Eghishē Ch'arents'[3]. Pulling from his pocket a slim volume published in Moscow, in a deep and passionate voice Shēms began to recite from Ch'arents'"s verse. Because he had known Ch'arents', he then told a few anecdotes, interjecting spirited comments of high praise. In fact, it later turned out that hearing those poems on that Sunday afternoon shaped Oshakan's own first impressions of Ch'arents'.

Immediately we were drawn to this rare and charismatic fellow who had only recently arrived from Romania. Barely thirty, a native of Trabzon, he had graduated from the Sanasarian Academy[4] and had then spent some years in the Caucasus.

Shēms possessed a wealth of memories from the many cities he had visited and lived in, especially recollections of all the writers, political activists and books he had come across. And he harbored strong opinions about each of them, whether expressed with a profuse, hearty affirmation or qualified by a deep, fervent disdain. A truly original thinker, he was always highly critical, restless of mind and independent in his views.

Although a Western Armenian, Shēms spoke Eastern Armenian. Well-versed in both branches of Armenian literature, he nevertheless felt closer in language, style, and aesthetics to Eastern Armenian writers. Given his natural, deep-seated tendency to be with common people, Shēms may well be regarded by some a proletarian voice.

From Cairo, Shēms went to Alexandria where, unable to pull himself away, he remained for the rest of his life; this city apparently was destined to become his final place of residence. More than once he had tried to flee;

he even had spent a couple of years in distant Paris, ostensibly to study the sciences of the occult as well as parapsychology, but unable to escape his fate, he would always return to Alexandria where his sheer presence brought the Armenian community to life; in turn, he seemed to find a certain happiness and contentment there, roosting in the attics of various houses in that most Europeanized of Arab cities.

Was there a single Armenian in Alexandria who did not come to know Shēms? Yet who was in fact this man, this poet who, according to his passport, was actually called Hmayeak Sap'rich'ian—a name I believe he, along with the authorities or possibly even others before them, had forgotten?

While it may have been difficult to locate Shēms out and about the city, it was never hard to recognize him.

If you should spot someone standing on a street corner, surrounded by a cadre of young men and talking incessantly of strange and mysterious things, someone who utters his good-bye but then lingers to keep talking even after only one of the group remains to listen, *that must be Shēms.*

Or if you should notice someone sitting in a corner of a café, hall or tavern, a solitary listener who takes deep pleasure in lighting one cigar after another, enveloped in smoke, and immersed in his own thoughts, *that must be Shēms.*

Or should you by chance see *someone* with slightly rounded shoulders, his head bent forward toward the ground, walking along a street without looking right or left and then stepping into a café or unpretentious bar to join the company of destitute men sitting among the noise, smoke and fumes, follow him: *that must be Shēms.* There he might remain for hours, often alone, occasionally with friends, a glass of ouzo, wine, or vermouth in front of him, which he will swill and savor in a familiar gesture and then ask to have refilled, all the while waving greetings to strangers of diverse origin seated nearby or off at a distance. Before long, he will cheerfully summon "Yani" or "Nikola," devising some Greek epithet as a gesture of endearment or friendship.

With his wide forehead extending all the way around both sides of his face, fully exposing the front of his brow, Shēms's long, fine silvery strands of thinning hair hung behind his head, forming a cluster on each side. He had a bony, striking and vivid countenance, with a prominent forehead and a solid curve outlining his temples; you might not even notice his wispy eyebrows until his eyes were fixed on you as a wave of consternation wrinkled his brow. His nose was firm and, together with his high cheekbones, conveyed something of his formidable character and strong will. His soul-stirring gaze, however, was a peaceful one, full of kindness, assuming a restrained complacence whenever he professed sympathy, recalled an old memory, described a fleeting dream, or recited a poem. He had a voice deep, seductive, intimate and warm—until, without warning, he might burst forth with lines from Sayat-Nova, his eyes narrowing and his face brightening into a broad smile:

> However much the wind may blow it away, there will be no lack of sand from the sea.
> Whether I be, or whether I be not, there will be no lack of music at court.
> If I am not there, am not there for you, not (as much as) a single hair will be lacking in this world.[5]

The excitement in his voice would heighten, or drop into an emphatic bass, as though a fragment had been released from his soul, so full of sorrow he would virtually break into tears. His whole world was the world of art, literature and philosophy, that realm of elusive, ever-changing horizons to which he was devoted and whose secrets he endeavored to analyze as a psychiatrist or spiritualist might.

During those precious, fascinating, tender moments, Shēms revealed his very essence—as an idealistic, high-minded, and truly Armenian soul. But his calm would last until someone raised a disturbing or distressing public concern, or alluded to the vanity of the rich and famous or those in authority and positions of power. Then his face would twist and bend in contortions, turning flush; his tone would become stern and prolonged, his scowl like lightning, his words harsh.

Still himself even when on stage, Shēms was adept at thrilling his audiences with the power of his ideas and the passion of his convictions, as he attacked all public indecencies, injustices and illegalities, turning each into an object of sharp derision.

A natural teacher, Shēms could often be found on the steps of a school or in a classroom, where he spoke to students enthusiastically about the beauties of the Armenian language and its literature, or of Armenian history—the glorious achievements of "the Armenian race." He lectured and taught everywhere, inside and outside classrooms, on streets or in cafés, on stages or in churchyards, even in homes, like one of Socrates' disciples, always surrounded by both his old and his new students who were mesmerized by him and who maintained their association with, and respect for, him even after becoming parents themselves.

Shēms was the paradigm of contradictions: he was rich in dreams yet meager in his ability simply to deal with everyday life; he was a devoted teacher and yet, as a poet, he defied rules and regulations; he cherished the fellowship of students as well as colleagues, yet he was constantly at odds with the authorities and others in seats of power; he may have been humble in life and work yet he was equally proud and steadfast in his convictions and ethics; a member of the Armenian Revolutionary Federation [Dashnak for short][6], he was always ready to throw himself into the fray, yet he was also friends with anti-Dashnaks, who knew him, sometimes persecuted him yet always respected him.

He was never comfortable with what he saw: people, his environs, the city, the working life, indeed the world itself, yet he embraced a simple chaste existence as his own. All he required was a modest meal, consisting of a few olives, a glass of beer, and a fish head, which he most enjoyed in the company of his own musings.

A delightful conversationalist, confidant and counselor, he could also remain silent for long spells, listening to perturbations of his soul. He would habitually observe his surroundings, looking off into the distance, watching people attentively and taking note of their wretched or sordid behavior. And he would scoff at the grandiose as much as at the petty. All the while Shēms preserved his greatest love for the meek, delighting in the company of humble folk and their straightforward talk.

Among his favorite poets was Omar Khayyam, ever present at his table:

> Ah, my Beloved, fill the Cup that clears
> Today of past Regrets and future Fears:
> Tomorrow!—Why, Tomorrow I may be
> Myself with Yesterday's Sev'n thousand Years.

Still, do not think of Shēms as a drunkard. To the contrary, he was a man who loved wine or ouzo in order to enjoy a few carefree moments, to remain above, so to speak, the mire of the world, the shabby affairs of mankind—and to share a toast or a table with those who were simple in spirit and noble in heart: the plain folk. For that reason, he counted more shoemakers, grocers, craftsmen and laborers among his friends than pundits and the so-called "power brokers," with whom his language remained imperious and his stance intransigent.

On the other hand, Shēms's writing is the poetry of pure spirit, the murmur of a restless soul. It is a cry of protest and rebellion, a quest for beauty and a dream, expressed in a powerful voice. His works include an array of prose and poetry, consisting of both original works and translations. It is, in short, unnecessary to label Shēms as either orator, poet, journalist, teacher, or political activist. Quite simply, he was all these things, with none overshadowing the others but all integral, inspired, genuine, unique and dynamic. Any literary work which voiced the spirit, or instilled the spirit, was acceptable to him.

Shēms cared little, in fact, for stringency of style, artistry, or any special embellishment of decorum and language. Vigor, faith and daring—these were the qualities he demanded in the expression of his ideas. At the core of his prose writings we find the Armenian nation, the Armenian people. His poetry, by contrast, sings of his perpetual anguish.

Indeed, the best way to portray Shēms is to think of the magnificent ruins of Armenian churches . . . He was an expatriate, a lone émigré in search of Mt Ararat and its shade, a man seeking the heart in others, a dreamer who longed to create the song of the heart.

Hmayeak Shēms was a dervish aspiring to be an artist, an artist living the life of the dervish.

Appendix B

The Hmayeak Shēms I Knew[1]

Step'an Shahpaz[2]

It has been almost a quarter century. I confess I do not recall the circumstances that threw us together in Alexandria. From the start we both sought out each other's company. Or so I believe. In this sense, our meetings may be taken as a testimony. Each time he entered my office, he proceeded toward me in measured steps, with a sharp, piercing gaze, a smile on the corner of his mouth, greeting me in the manner we usually expect of clerics: "Greetings unto you!" We may well think of him as our lay cleric, a priest, regardless of his religious convictions.

From the first I knew him to be a teacher and writer, as well as a member of the Dashnak party. He, in turn, was equally aware of my politics.[3] Yet we never discussed any political issues that might divide us. Our meetings were never unduly restrained, nor, in fact, were they very frequent.

He treasured the Armenian language and literature. His eyes sparkled whenever he spoke of them. He had nurtured our language. His love for Armenian was profound and passionate. Indeed, this fact was the basis for our mutual regard.

Shēms had both followers and enemies. It would be unlikely, indeed impossible, to believe that such a man of ideas, one given to expressing himself candidly and fearlessly, would have only friends, only sympathizers.

And, of course, Shēms had his faults—human frailties—just as everyone does. Any other man of his temperament, ideas, sensitivity, would have easily succumbed to them. But those shortcomings harmed himself more than others, and sadly so. He drank; he poisoned himself a little each day. He may have had his reasons for it. Or maybe his drinking was an act of fate. A rebellion.

He was an intellectual and he was proud. I admired his pride; that feeling prevailed in him. He was proud as a teacher, even as a party advocate. He never gave up. He never tolerated a party policy that did not make sense to him. Nor did he ever deny his party affiliation, nor his biases, very much like a man of faith; even there he maintained his integrity. One simply had to know him for who he was.

The topic of our conversations was usually Armenian literature or language, and on occasion we would discuss the nature of the Armenian character.

Surprisingly, all those years, Shēms would never bring up national politics, nor would I. At the time I did not ask myself why not. I do not think it was a deliberate avoidance by either of us. To this day, I suspect the only reason was, undoubtedly, our respect for each other's views. In any case, Armenian literature gave us plenty to talk about. Still, I want to emphasize here this unusual circumstance in order to press a point: differences in opinion need not be grounds for splitting people apart, nor need they cause two people to turn against each other.

I believe Shēms greatly enjoyed visiting me. He obviously had no obligation to do so. And he knew I shared this pleasure. To talk about Armenian literature was all he needed to do; his love for it ran very deep indeed. More than once he read to me from his writings, some published, some unpublished. Our bond was based on the fact that I, too, revere Armenian language and literature. And this reverence played no small part in our high regard for one another. To the contrary, I dare say it made for an even stronger friendship.

One who did not know Shēms might have thought that he did not believe in his own ideas and basic premises. Whenever he spoke, between his words lurked a sardonic grin, a grin that could have easily misled people. But they would have been wrong. In truth, nothing could get him to abandon his convictions.

Obviously, his was an embittered soul. Overall, Armenian teachers, writers, and Armenian people in general were not much appreciated. This, of course, was nothing new, neither for him nor for me. We have had many embittered teachers and writers among us; in fact, so commonplace is this sad situation as to be hardly worth mentioning. Shēms used to believe that only flatterers succeed in life. And under no circumstances would he want to be numbered among them. He never was. He complained with a sunken heart even about his own party's bosses. He always maintained an independent stance vis-à-vis the party elite, showing disdain toward any policies dictated from the top tier. He would never betray his own principles.

To be sure, we Armenians need to be more tolerant of each other. We are not accustomed to being so. We judge prematurely, without first examining a situation carefully and listening to others. We tend to think that all people are born of the same mold: that they all have the same brain, same heart, and same reactions. In Shēms the sense of pride had an Armenian muscle. But this was not born out of conceit nor from a *complexe de supériorité*. To the contrary, it emerged from the keen sensitivities of the true intellectual, a truly human being. From this perspective, he never yielded. He remained proud while at the same time modest, very modest, to the degree that he was entirely democratic, even to the point of becoming a dervish. In fact, he wrote about the dervish.

Armenians may boast of many patriots among themselves. In this respect, too, the standards are relative. But Shēms's patriotism was one of his most fundamental and unyielding characteristics. Only once did I hear him speak in public on the subject, during a mass meeting held to promote Armenian repatriation from abroad to the homeland. His speech dwarfed the most ardent of speeches or writings by others on the subject. He said what no one had dared say or could say. Therein resounded the quintessence of patriotism; and he expressed himself freely, without restraint, subject only to the cries of his heart.

Our relationship, namely our friendship, did not veer beyond this path. But I regarded the contact we had, and still regard it, as centrally important to my own life.

For instance, Shēms would delve into great detail about the etymology or usage of a word, or the construction of a sentence; he doted on and cared for them as if they were his own children. His devotion to the Armenian language gave me a great deal of pleasure, for I, too, have shared this devotion, this love. Shēms's own beautiful style of writing undoubtedly emerged from this concern and love for the Armenian language.

Consequently, during our meetings none of our differences surfaced. I am not suggesting, nor have I ever professed, that ideology can be avoided in literature. But, surely, it is possible to cultivate the Armenian language and to debate it without letting partisanship, political or otherwise, interfere. Moreover, it is even possible to maintain mutual respect while freely exchanging opposing political views.

In recent years, the papers and letters of Romain Rolland have begun to be published in rather large volumes. The second of these contains letters he wrote to Louis Gillet, together with the letters he received from the latter.[4] Between these two French intellectuals had always existed irreconcilable ideological differences, from their earliest acquaintance as young men; but they nonetheless remained friends until old age. Their later letters in particular are touching and provide an excellent model of the largesse of the heart for all readers, especially for us Armenians. Sadly, this kind of friendship rarely exists among Armenians, if it exists at all, particularly when individuals stubbornly cling to their separate views. I am beginning to believe that we Armenians simply prefer not to respect the views of our fellow Armenians, perhaps seeing in that respect our own belittlement.

The invitation to record these reflections on Shēms came from his nephew, Vahé Baladouni, who is himself an independent thinker and who intends through publication to pass on Shēms's legacy—his poetry and prose writings—to future generations.[5] Others, I am sure, will write about Shēms as a teacher and writer. I, from my limited contact with him, and in taking an independent departure, would like to reiterate here that only from a true love for Armenian literature, and only with intellectuals who respect each other, can we create, *must* we create, an atmosphere in which our long-suffering people can finally and fully benefit, throughout the diaspora. By stressing this point, I hope to perpetuate a cherished memory from Hmayeak Shēms.

Appendix C

An Undated Draft Letter to Levon Hovhannēsian Written by Hmayeak Shēms Regarding Three Modes of Rendering Khach'atur Abovian's *Verk' Hayastani* into Western Armenian

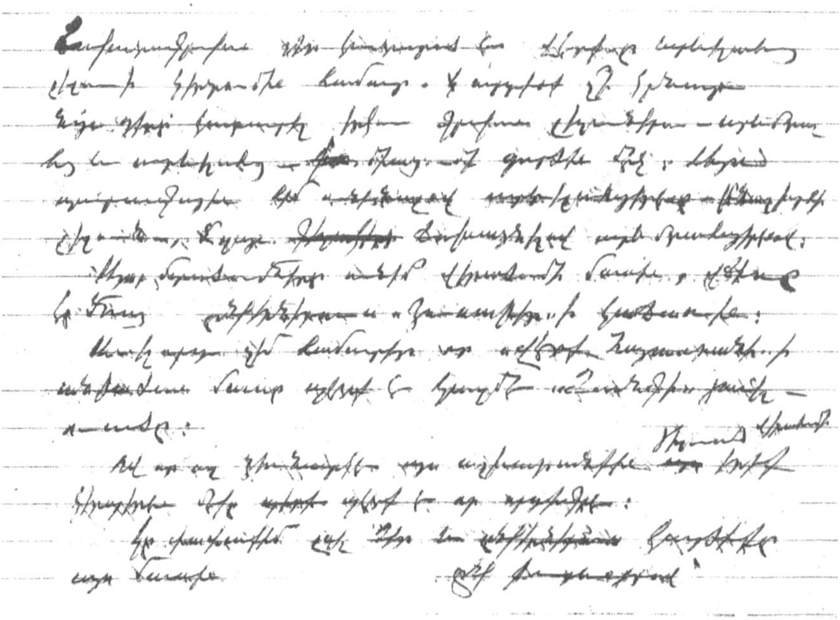

The English translation of this letter follows:

Dear Mr Levon Hovhannēsian,

Mr Herartian, on your behalf, has asked me to undertake a rendition of [Khach'atur Abovian's[1]] *Verk' Hayastani* into Western Armenian and let you know my terms. I have done so. Aside from the fact that no action has yet been taken on the matter, I would like here to summarize my thoughts on three possible approaches to the task:

Rendition of Verk' Hayastani into Western Armenian literary idiom. Such a rendition would undoubtedly lose much of the "blazing passion" and "flavor" of the original novel, especially the poems, which form a considerable part of the work.

Modernizing it in today's Eastern Armenian idiom. By adopting Ṛaffi's or Aharonian's literary style, such a rendition could not only help maintain most of the authenticity and beauty of the original, but would also be accessible to Western Armenians.

Considering a third way of rendition. Verk' has played a foreordained role in the formation of Eastern Armenian. Could it not, perhaps, play a similar role in splicing the Eastern and Western literary idioms? In that case, we could take as its basic idiom Eastern Armenian—the language of our homeland—and then enrich it with the idiom unique to Western Armenian.[2]

These are my thoughts on the matter. The verdict remains with the members of the *Houssaper* [Husaber] Academy.[3]

Needless to say, the addendum [to *Verk'*], entitled *Zang*, should be considered as an integral part of *Verk' Hayastani*.

Whoever undertakes the rendition, one must choose one of the above three approaches to the task.

I would like to hear your own, as well as my friends'[4] thoughts on this matter.

With friendly regards,

Notes

PREFACE

1. Eghishē Ch'arents' (1897-1937), Armenian poet, achieved prominence in Soviet Armenia with his revolutionary spirit and intense creative quest. During the early years of sovietization, Ch'arents' served in the Red Army. Several volumes of his works have been published, most notably his two collections of poetry, *The Epic Dawn* (1930) and *The Book of Voyage* (1933). He has influenced generations of Armenian poets.

PART I

1. Hmayyag [Hmayeak] Shems [Shēms], *For the House of Torkom* [T'orgom], trans. Vahé Baladouni and John Gery (Merrick, NY: Cross-Cultural Communications, 1999) 35.

2. Gurgēn Mkhit'arian, "A Portrait of Hmayyag [Hmayeak] Shems [Shēms]," trans. Vahé Baladouni and John Gery, *Ararat* [New York] Spring 1999: 17. The original text appeared in *Hairenik* [Hayrenik'] *Daily* [Boston] 3 May 1952: 1. Unless otherwise indicated, all subsequent unnumbered quotations are from this memoir. See Appendix A.

3. Mkhit'arian 18. We are reminded here of Robert Burns' "My Heart's in the Highlands," one of the many poetic expressions of the power inherent in the homeland. Poets have, from times immemorial, sung the holiness of the homeland and the painful existence away from home. With our apologies to Robert Burns (1759-1796), we give below a rearranged version of his song:

> My heart's in the Highlands, my heart is not here;
> My heart's in the Highlands, wherever I go.

> Wherever I wander, wherever I rove,
> The hills of the Highlands forever I love.

4. "Mer Korustnerĕ" [Our Losses], editorial, *Houssaper* [Husaber] *Daily* [Cairo] 24 May 1952: 1.

5. Place-names of the city of Alexandria are given in their original French spelling.

6. Hovakim Hovakimian (Arshakuni), *Patmut'iwn Haykakan Pontosi* [History of the Armenian Pontus] (Beirut: Mshak, 1967) 28.

7. Hovakimian, 552-53.

8. Aregents' H., "Meṛats tghu mĕ tetrakĕ" [Notebook of a Deceased Boy], *Houssaper* [Husaber] *Daily* [Cairo] 7 June 1941.

9. Hovakimian, 28.

10. Aregents'.

11. H. Arshakuni (Hovakim Hovakimian), "Hmayeak Shēms—taghandavor dervishĕ" [Hmayeak Shēms: the Talented Dervish], Unpublished memoir, 2. Unless otherwise indicated, all subsequent unnumbered quotations are from this memoir.

12. The story of Armenia's conversion from paganism to Christianity is a fascinating one, full of high drama, awaiting to be told perhaps by a novelist, playwright, or filmmaker, or by all three. See: Sirarpie Der Nersessian, *The Armenians* (New York: Praeger Publishers, 1970) 72-78; George A. Bournoutian, *A Concise History of the Armenian People* (Costa Mesa, CA: Mazda Publishers, Inc., 2002) 47-48.

13. Arshakuni, 2-3.

14. East of Istanbul and west of Erevan, the children of the Armenian elite were often educated in largely anglophone missionary schools after receiving their elementary education in Armenian schools. Sanasarian Academy was the sole equivalent to the great Armenian lycées of Istanbul. On Sanasarian Academy, see Pamela J. Young, "The Sanasarian Varzharan: Making a People into a Nation" in Richard G. Hovannisian, ed., *Armenian Karin/Erzerum* (Costa Mesa, CA: Mazda Publishers, 2003) 261-81.

15. For a biographical write-up, see Hovakimian, 119-21.

16. Hovakimian, 196-99.

17. Arshakuni, 6.

18. H. Shēms, "Erek' varpetner" [Three Masters], *Houssaper* [Husaber] *Daily* [Cairo] 24 April 1948. Unless otherwise indicated, all subsequent unnumbered quotations are from this memoir.

19. The reference here is to Vahan Tērian's first book of poetry, *Mtnshaghi Anurjner* [Twilight Reveries], published in 1908.

20. A somewhat different version of these events is given in Ghazar-Ch'areg, *Karinapatum* (Beirut: Mshak, 1957) 222-31.

21. Later scholars have found important correspondences between Nietzsche's and Buddhist writings. Among others, see: Graham Parkes, "The Early Reception of Nietzsche's Philosophy in Japan," in Graham Parks, ed., *Nietzsche and Asian Thought* (Chicago: University of Chicago Press, 1991) 177-99; Graham Parkes, "Nietzsche and East Asian Thought: Influences, Impacts, and Resonances," in Bernd Magnus and Kathleen Higgins, eds., *The Cambridge Companion to Nietzsche* (Cambridge: Cambridge University Press, 1996) 356-83.

22. "Gēvorgian Academy," *Haykakan hamaṛot hanragitaran* [Concise Armenian Encyclopedia], 1990 ed.

23. At the time, the Holy See at Ējmiatsin announced the cause of death as "heart failure." However, given the strained state-church relations in Armenian SSR of the period, it was widely believed that Khorēn Kat'oghikos had been murdered by the infamous Beria's secret police (later the KGB). During the period 1936-1938 Stalin's oppression had reached its peak. Leading members of the Communist Party and state officials were prime targets, but no one was safe. Wild denunciations and arbitrary arrests were commonplace.

24. Arsēn Tērtērian, *Vahan Tērian: ts'nork'i, tsaravi ew hashtut'ean ergich'ē* [Vahan Tērian: Poet of Delusion, Thirst, and Harmony] (Tiflis: Hermes, 1910) 91 and *passim*.

25. H. Shēms, "Inch'u ayrvets'an?" [Why Did They Get Burned?], *Houssaper* [Husaber] *Daily* [Cairo] 28 August 1948.

26. H. Shēms, "Ur kert'a metsask'anch'ē?" [Metsask'anch': Quo Vadis?], *Houssaper* [Husaber] *Daily* [Cairo] 2 July 1938.

27. Step'an Shahpaz, "Hmayeak Shēmsē zor chanch'ts'a" [The Hmayeak Shēms I Knew], *Horizon Literary Supplement* [Montreal] January 2002: 14. Unless otherwise indicated, all subsequent unnumbered quotations are from this memoir. See Appendix B.

28. On the Armenian Genocide, see: Vahakn N. Dadrian, *The History of the Armenian Genocide* (Providence, RI: Berghahn Books, 1995); *Genocide and Human Rights: Lessons from the Armenian Experience* (A special issue of the Journal of Armenian Studies), Volume IV, Nos. 1 and 2: 1992; Richard G. Hovannisian, *The Armenian Holocaust: A Bibliography Relating to the Deportations, Massacres, and Dispersion of the Armenian People, 1915-1923* (Cambridge, MA: Armenian Heritage Press, 1980); Robert W. Thomson, ed., *Recent Studies in Modern Armenian History* (Cambridge, MA: Armenian Heritage Press, 1972).

29. On Armenian history, see: Richard G. Hovannisian, ed., *The Armenian People: from Ancient to Modern Times*, 2 vols. (New York: St Martin's Press, 1997); George A. Bournoutian, *A Concise History of the Armenian People: from Ancient Times to the Present* (Costa Mesa, CA: Mezda Publishers, 2002); David Marshall Lang, *Armenia: Cradle of Civilization* (London: George Allen and Unwin, 1973).

30. Arshakuni.

31. Ervand Fntk'ian, Unpublished memoir, 24 February 1953, 2.

32. In 1922, Garegin Vardapet Khach'aturian (1880-1961), a cleric of distinction and a man of letters, was ordained bishop in Ējmiatsin by His Holiness Gēvorg V, Kat'oghikos of All Armenians. In 1937, he was bestowed the title of "archbishop" and in 1950 was elected to the see of the Patriarchate of Constantinople. Hovakimian, *Patmut'iwn Haykakan Pontosi*, 562-64, 295-99; "Hangist" [RIP], *Ējmiatsin* August 1961: 8-9. *Note*: In a letter dated 31 January 2007, addressed to Vahé Baladouni, Fr Krikor H. Maksoudian provides the following historical information on the use of the title of "archbishop" in the Armenian Church:

> At present, 'archbishop' is merely an honorary title in our church. The kat'oghikos bestows it on a bishop with an encyclical, which is usually read in church during liturgy or a special ceremony, neither of which is liturgically or canonically required. In ancient times, the Armenian Church did not use the title. Its earliest use seems to date from the

Bagratid period (around 10th-11th cc). There is, however, even an earlier reference in a hierarchical list from the 8th century, which recognizes it as a rank allegedly and theoretically held by the head of the Church of Caucasian Albania. During the Cilician period (11th-14th cc), the bishops of important bishoprics were referred to as 'archbishops.' This tradition of giving a higher rank to the bishop of an important see probably had its origin in Bagratid times. During the 19th and 20th cc, the title was given to (1) the bishops who were elevated to the rank of patriarch of Jerusalem and Constantinople; (2) elderly bishops who had served the church for many years; and (3) primates of large dioceses. This custom is still in force.

33. Garegin Archbishop Khach'aturian, letter to Vahé Baladouni, 30 October 1952.

34. Gurgēn Ter-Vardanian, letter to Vahé Baladouni, 18 February 1953: 3-5.

35. Vardan Gēvorgian, Unpublished memoir, 16 November 1952: 1-2. Unless otherwise indicated, all subsequent unnumbered quotations are from this memoir. Gēvorgian has published two volumes of poetry, *Tsovun Ergĕ* [Song of the Sea] and *Voski Sap'or* [Golden Urn] as well as a book entitled *Grakan Harts'er* [Literary Issues]. During his nineteen years in Buenos Aires, he edited *Armenia*, a daily newspaper.

36. Komitas Vardapet, born Soghomon Soghomonian (1869-1935), was one of the most tragic victims of the Armenian Genocide. As an eyewitness to the genocide, Komitas suffered mental breakdown and in 1916, through the intervention of influential figures, was taken to a psychiatric clinic in suburban Paris, where he remained for the rest of his life. In 1936 his remains were transported to Erevan, and in 1948 the Erevan Conservatory was renamed after him. A founder of the Armenian ethnological studies, he was educated at the Gevorgian Theological Seminary (Gēvorgian Academy) in Vagharshapat (now Ējmiatsin) and later attended Professor Richard Schmidt's Conservatory in Berlin. He devoted his life to the study of Armenian folk music, interpreting its distinctive characteristics and producing his own treatment of native folk songs. One of his major works is *Patarag* [Divine Liturgy], still used today as one of two most popular settings of the Armenian Church liturgy. Composer, scholar, choral conductor, musicologist, ethnologist, pedagogue, and public figure, he is perhaps best remembered as a major contributor to the national school of Armenian music. "Komitas," *Haykakan hamaŗot hanragitaran* [Armenian Concise Encyclopedia], Erevan, Armenia, 1995. See also: "Komitas Vardapet," *The New Grove Dictionary of Music and Musicians*, 2001 ed. and Robert At'ayan, et al. "Komitas Vardapet," Grove Music Online. Oxford Music Online. 28 July 2008.

37. As quoted by Gēvorgian, 2-3.

38. *Navasard: Journal of Literature and Art* [Bucharest] October 1923. In 1914 Siruni and the noted Armenian poet Daniel Varuzhan (1884-1915) published a yearbook of literature and art under the name *Navasard*. Comprised of some 340 pages, the publication had brought together the works of some of the most distinguished Eastern and Western Armenian writers and intellectuals. In the following year, Daniel Varuzhan became a victim of the 1915 Armenian Genocide. Hakob Siruni (1890-1973) somehow survived the genocide and in 1923 revived the yearbook as a periodical, serving as its sole editor. It ceased publication in 1926.

39. H. Ch. Siruni, "K'ani me dēmk'er vor kĕ banan serundĕ" [A Few Figures that Usher In the New Generation] *Haratch Daily* [Paris] 17 November 1929. Reprinted in *Haratch-50*, a commemorative anthology published on the occasion of the

newspaper's 50th anniversary (Paris: Haratch Press, 1976) 30-35. This article was brought to the authors' attention by the late Misak Tölölyan, writer; the full citation was provided by his son, Khachik Tölölyan, editor, *Diaspora: A Journal of Transnational Studies*.

PART II

1. Hovakimian, 483.
2. Atmachian's letter, together with her autographed book of poetry, was lost in Hurricane Katrina. Marie's brother, Gegham At'machian (1910-1940), pen name Sema, was also a poet. He died in World War II in the defense of France.
3. Hovakimian, 482-83.
4. Hovakimian, 481-82.
5. Hovakimian, 482-83.
6. On Ch'arents', see note to the Preface.
7. Mkhit'arian, 15.
8. Founded by Alexander the Great in 332 BCE, this city on the Mediterranean coast of Egypt was, under Ptolemaic rule (323-30 BCE), a renowned center of literature, science, and mathematics. During the Roman and Byzantine Periods (30 BCE–642 CE), philosophy flourished there, and with the spread of Christianity it became an intellectual hub of the Christian world. Under Arab and Turkish rule (642-1798 CE), however, Alexandria lost its former prestigious standing and by the time Napoleon landed at nearby Abuqir Bay in 1798, it was no more than a fishing village. On ancient Alexandria, see: Justin Pollard and Howard Reid, *The Rise and Fall of Alexandria: Birthplace of the Modern Mind* (New York: Viking, 2006).
9. The cosmopolitan Alexandria that Shēms came to know is superbly described by the English novelist E. M. Forster (1879-1970) in his now classic guidebook entitled *Alexandria: A History and a Guide* (Alexandria: W. Morris Limited, 1922). Written during World War I and later revised, this non-fiction book is Forster's tribute to Alexandria, which has haunted and inspired its visitors for over two millennia. There have been several hardback and paperback editions since its first publication.
10. Evelyn Baring (Earl of Cromer), *Modern Egypt* (New York: The Macmillan Company, 1908, 1909; reprinted in 2000), Vol. II, 220.
11. Hovhannes Khach'iki T'op'uzyan, *Egiptosi Haykakan Gaghut'i Patmut'yun (1805-1952)* [A History of the Armenian Community of Egypt] (Erevan: Haykakan SSH GA Hratarakch'ut'yun, 1978), Chapter Three.
12. H. Amirian, "Hmayeak Shēms," *Houssaper* [Husaber] *Daily* [Cairo] Exact date unavailable, 1952.
13. As quoted by Gēvorgian. Elsewhere in his memoir, Gēvorgian writes: "I have some fifteen letters from Shēms, each of which opens a window onto his tormented soul. One can hardly get to know Shēms without having read those letters." The letters referred to have not been available to us. However, the extracts quoted from those letters by Gēvorgian in his memoir give us a fair feel for Shēms's continuing spiritual turmoil.
14. The art songs of Srvandztiants'and those of other composers on the lyrics of Hmayeak Shēms were later compiled and republished in a 120-page musical opus,

entitled *Erger Hmayeak Shēmsi Khosk'erov* [Songbook on the Lyrics of Hmayeak Shēms, 2001].

15. Henri Durville (1888-1963), psychotherapist and author of some fifty books, was founder of the International Psychical Society and editor of *Journal du Magnétisme*. His works include *La Science Secrète* [The Secret Science, 1923], *Mystères Initiatiques* [Initiatic Mysteries, 1929], *La Magie Divine* [Divine Magic, 1930], *Cours de Magnétisme Personnel* [Course in Personal Magnetism, 1933]. "Durville, Henri," *Encyclopedia of Occultism and Parapsychology*, 1984 ed.

16. *Buzhank': Aṛoghjapahakan, gitakan ew enkerayin amsagir*, Vol. 4 (January-March 1929).

17. As quoted by Gēvorgian, 5.

18. As quoted by Gēvorgian, 5.

19. Victoria Arsharuni, "An Autobiographical Sketch," *Arev* [Cairo] 6 September 1971.

20. Unfinished, undated letter from Shēms to Hovakimian, never mailed. Years later, in 1956, upon his arrival to the United States to pursue his higher education, Vahé Baladouni visited with Hovakim Hovakimian who, at the time, lived in Royal Oak, Michigan, and handed the aforesaid letter to him in person. Unless otherwise indicated, all subsequent unnumbered quotations are from this letter.

21. Vardan Gēvorgian, "Glukh glkhi Shēmsin het" [Tête-à-Tête with Shēms], *Armenia* [Buenos Aires] 12 November 1959.

22. As quoted by Gēvorgian, Unpublished memoir, 5-6.

23. Sayat'-Nova, *Khagher: Liakatar Zhoghovatsu* [Sayat-Nova, Songs: Complete Works] ed. Henrik Bakhch'inian, (Erevan, Armenia: Museum of Literature and Art, 2003) 5.

24. Sayat'-Nova, 301-42.

25. The script for the Armenian language was invented by Mesrop Mashtots', a learned cleric, in 405 CE, aided by Sahak the Great, supreme head of the Armenian Apostolic Church. For more than 1600 years the Armenian language has served as a critical component of Armenian identity. It has survived the imperial rule of Persia, Rome, Byzantium, the Ottoman Empire, and most recently the Soviet Union. While other ancient languages have become obsolete or evolved into other languages, Classical Armenian (*Grabar*) has evolved into a vibrant modern vernacular.

26. Perch Momchian, "Chashka chaï," *Horizon* [Montreal] 30 March 1992: 9-12.

27. Shahpaz, 13-14.

28. Andranik Tsaṛukian, review of *Hay grakanut'iwn* [Armenian Literature] by H. Oshakan, *Nayiri* (Aleppo, Syria: Ter-Sahakian Press, 1942), Vol. I, No.5, 276-280. Hṛomayets'i, "To the Attention of the Historian: Attestations," *Arev* [Cairo] 1 April 1957.

29. Armēn Nayiri, "Im p'ilisop'a usuts'ich's" [My Philosopher-Teacher], *Houssaper* [Husaber] *Daily* [Cairo] Exact date unavailable, 1952.

30. Ṛozin Manukian, "Ert'as barov im sireli usuts'ich's Shēms" [Farewell, My Dear Teacher Shēms], *Araxe* [Arak's] *Weekly* [Alexandria] 19 April 1952.

31. Rev Fr Haykazun Voskerich'ian, letter to Vahé Baladouni, 25 August 1954.

32. Momchian, 10.

33. The *kemancha* is a four-stringed musical instrument played with a bow. The sound box is usually made of walnut tree wood and has the shape of a parabola.

When being played, the instrument is held in upright position. Contrary to the violin, it is the string that moves along the bow as the instrument is turned on its spike. The *kemancha* is held by the neck with the left hand and bowed with the right. Used as a solo instrument for singing, dancing, and sheer listening, it was a favorite of the eighteenth-century *gusans* (troubadours) such as Sayat-Nova. The State Museum of History in Armenia has in its collection an eighteenth-century *kemancha* from Tiflis, Georgia, said to have been played by Sayat-Nova himself. Levon Abrahamian and Nancy Sweezy, eds., *Armenian Folk Arts, Culture, and Identity* (Bloomington, IN: Indiana University Press, 2001), 238; also 235, 243, 272.

34. Gēvorgian, 7.

35. Author of *Erb Erkink'ĕ Anoghok' Ē* [When the Sky Is Ruthless] and *Gorsh Gaylĕ Katgher Ēr* [The Dreaded Wolf Gone Wild], among others. In his novel, *Pahakĕ Patnēshin Vra* [The Guard on the Rampart], T'agvorian casts Shēms as a character under the pseudonym H. Shoghuni (*shogh* means "ray" or "sunray" in Armenian; *uni*, an Armenian proper name ending meaning "has"), 90-92 and 190-210. T'agvorian had also prepared a manuscript entitled *Contemporary Figures: A Literary-Psychological Essay* on five literary figures: Intra [Indra], N. Aghbalian, Hakob Oshakan, Hamastegh, and Hm. Shēms, identifying each writer by his dominant literary characteristic. The chapter devoted to Shēms's œuvre is entitled *Depi Vogeghinats'um* [Toward Spiritualization]. The announcement of this manuscript appeared on the back cover of T'agvorian's *Gorsh Gaylĕ Katgher Ēr*. We have been unable to ascertain whether it was eventually published or not.

36. The name Nayiri stands for both a geographic area around Lake Van in Eastern Anatolia and its people. It is derived from the word "nayir," meaning country between rivers in Assyrian. Situated north of Mesopotamia, between the Euphrates and Tigris, Nayiri resisted Assyrian and Hittite domination during the late Bronze Age. However, by the 11th century BCE its influence waned as a related tribe, the Urartians, came to power. The Urartians were eventually succeeded in the 6th century BCE by the Armenians. Armenians see Nayiri as one of their most ancient ancestors. Since late 19th century CE, Armenian poets, such as Terian, Ch'arents', and Shēms, have come to use the name Nayiri as a synonym for Armenia.

37. Gēvorgian, 6.

38. The translators have taken the liberty of modifying the original title of this prose poem, which literally translates into "A Vision for the House of T'orgom."

39. Among Shēms's surviving manuscripts we find the outline of a three-act play (untitled).

40. Shahpaz, 13.

41. *Hairenik* [Hayrenik'] *Daily* [Boston] 21 September 1975.

42. *Hairenik* [Hayrenik'] *Daily* [Boston] 23 November 1975.

43. Mkhit'arian, 17.

44. Because of his failing health, Shēms dictated this letter, dated 24 March 1951, to his nephew, Vahé, who transcribed it in longhand.

45. Hmayeak Shēms, *Erker* [Selected Works], ed. Henrik Bakhch'inian (Erevan, Armenia: Eghishē Ch'arents' Museum of Literature and Art, 2002) 16.

46. Gēvorg K'ristinian, review of *Hmayeak Shēms: Entir Erker*, *Asbarez* [Asparēz] 4 April 1995: 15. See also K'ristinian's letter dated 5 January 1995 to Vahé Baladouni.

APPENDIX A

1. Editor of several major Armenian newspapers and literary magazines in the Diaspora, Gurgēn Mkhit'arian (1890-1962) is noted for his literary criticism. He has translated French literature, including Zola, into Armenian. Twice imprisoned during the period of the Armenian Genocide, he finally escaped Turkey and came to Egypt in 1922 where he assumed the editorship of *Houssaper Daily* and *Houssaper Literary Monthly*. In 1948 he moved to the United States and assumed the editorship of *Hairenik Daily* in Boston, Massachusetts, where he wrote this essay.

2. A prolific writer, Hakob Oshakan (1883-1937) produced many short stories, fables, novelettes, novels, and plays. He also worked tirelessly as a bibliographer of Armenian literature and had an illustrious career as a teacher.

3. On Eghishē Ch'arents' see the footnote to the Preface.

4. As it is evident from the biography, Shēms did not graduate from Sanasarian Academy.

5. Charles J. F. Dowsett, *Sayat-Nova: an 18th–century troubadour; a biographical and literary study* (Lovanii, In Aedibus Peeters, 1997), 99.

6. Founded in 1890 in Tiflis, Georgia, the Armenian Revolutionary Federation had as its goal the safeguard of the economic and political freedom of the Armenian people living in the Ottoman Empire.

APPENDIX B

1. This memoir, written in March 1955, was first published some forty-six years later in the Armenian newspaper *Harach* [Paris] April 21-22, 2001. In the following year, it was reprinted in the "Literary Supplement" of *Horizon Weekly* [Montreal] January 2002: 13-14. Here it receives its first English translation.

2. A well-known Armenian writer, Step'an Shahpaz (1900-1994) was born in Adana, Turkey. He received his early education at his hometown's Abgarian School. Later he went on to earn a law degree from the University of Paris. In 1926 he moved to Alexandria, Egypt. A highly regarded attorney and a prolific writer, he has contributed to Armenian newspapers and authored several books, including two novels *Varaguyrin etevĕ* [Behind the Curtain] (1946) and *Orerun het* [Our Days] (1970); a study on Armenian character, entitled *Menk' Hayers* [We, Armenians] (1959); a biographical and literary study on *Grigor Zohrap* (1959); and a French language work on the Armenians in Egypt (1966).

3. Though not a registered member, Shahpaz was a sympathizer of the conservative Armenian Democratic Liberal Party (Ramkavar), who accepted Soviet rule of Armenia as "an inevitable and beneficial step toward ensuring eventual independence by providing a great-power mandate over the beleaguered Armenians." By contrast, Shēms was a member of the Armenian Revolutionary Federation (Dashnak Party), "who espoused a nationalist and irredentist cause, [believing that] the destiny of the Armenians lay only in a free and independent Armenia." For more on the major political lines drawn between these two parties, see: Robert Mirak, "The Armenians in America," in Richard G. Hovannisian, ed., *The Armenian People from Ancient to Modern Times*, Vol. II, New York, 1997, 402-6.

4. *Correspondance entre Louis Gillet et Romain Rolland,* Paris, A. Michel, 1949. Romain Rolland (1866-1944), French novelist, playwright, biographer, musicologist, and Nobel Prize winner (1915) for his novel cycle *Jean Christophe* (1904-1912) and pacifist manifestos collected in *Au-dessus de la mêlée* (1915). Louis Gillet (1876-1943), art critic and member of the French Academy, is well known for his numerous books on French and Italian art.

5. Owing to the literary executor's departure from Egypt in 1956, the publication of Hmayeak Shēms's works was delayed until 1994.

APPENDIX C

1. Poet, novelist, essayist, playwright, folklorist, pedagogue, teacher, Khach'atur Abovian (1809-1849) was born in K'anak'er, near Erevan, now a suburb of the Armenian capital. He received his early education at the seminary in Ējmiatsin and at the Nersesian Academy in Tiflis. He then attended the University of Dorpat (now Tartu, Estonia) studying a wide range of subjects. Upon his return to Tiflis in 1837, he was appointed supervisor of the city's school district. In 1843 he moved to Erevan where he occupied a similar post until his mysterious disappearance in 1848. Abovian launched his literary career at a time when Armenian literature was still imbued in religious thought and the clergy was trying to keep the moribund classical language, *Grabar*, alive. Much as he loved classical Armenian and wrote in that idiom, he also knew too well that it was quickly becoming a dead language and hence the need for a vernacular, *ashkharhabar*. The exigency for a vernacular finally drove him to write his chef-d'oeuvre, *Verk' Hayastani* [Wounds of Armenia], a unique historical novel of epic proportions, in the spoken language of his birthplace. Published in Tiflis in 1858, ten years after his disappearance, it has earned its author the distinction as the founder of modern Eastern Armenian literature.

2. It is regrettable that this proposal was never pursued. Shēms was uniquely situated to undertake the task in this third manner. As Bakhch'inian notes, "As a creative writer, Shēms's language is a most unique fusion of Eastern and Western Armenian literary idioms."

3. Shēms fondly referred to the editorial staff of *Houssaper* as the Academy.

4. The reference here is to the editorial staff of *Houssaper*, including Gurgēn Mkhit'arian, Liparit Nazariants', and Benyamin T'ashian.

Acronyms and Abbreviations

ARF   Armenian Revolutionary Federation
BCE   before the common era
CE   common era
MLA   Eghishē Ch'arents' Museum of Literature and Art, Erevan, Armenia

Selected Bibliography

PRIMARY WORKS

Shēms, Hmayeak. *Roshnakan* [Luminous]. Alexandria, Egypt: A. Step'anian Press, 1943. Includes essays, prose poems, and poetry.

———. *Sayat'-Nova: Matean imastut'ean, geghets'kut'ean ew anmatuyts' siroy* [Book of Wisdom, Beauty, and Unrequited Love]. Alexandria, Egypt: A. Step'anian Press, 1944. A study of Sayat-Nova's life and works. Includes sixty of Nova's Armenian songs with lexical annotations; the musical score of eight of the most popular songs; a rich glossary of nearly one thousand two hundred words and phrases; and a rendition of twenty of Nova's best known songs into Western Armenian.

REPUBLISHED PRIMARY WORKS

Shēms, Hmayeak. *Erger Hmayeak Shēmsi khosk'erov* [Songs on the Lyrics of Hmayeak Shēms]. Comp. by Vahé Baladouni. Erevan, Armenia: Grakanut'ean ew arvesti t'angaran, 2001.

———. *Ěntir erker*. Edited by Vahé Baladouni. Watertown, MA: Baikar Publications, 1994. For a complete bibliography of Shēms's works, see pages 347-60.

———. *Erker*. Edited by Henrik Bakhch'inian. Erevan, Armenia: Grakanut'ean ew arvesti t'angaran, 2002.

———. *For the House of Torkom* [Prose Poems]. Translated by Vahé Baladouni and John Gery. Merrick, NY: Cross-Cultural Communications, 1999.

———. *Patmut'iwn hay grakanut'ean* [History of Armenian Literature]. Edited by Henrik Bakhch'inian. Erevan, Armenia: Grakanut'ean ew arvesti t'angaran, 2002.

———. "Sayat'-Novayi taghēre," *Sayat'-Nova: Matean imastut'ean, geghets'kut'ean ew anmatuyts' siroy* ["Songs of Sayat-Nova," Sayat-Nova: Book of Wisdom, Beauty and Unrequited Love] in *Sayat'-Nova: Khagher (Liakatar zhoghovatsu)*, ed. Henrik

Bakhch'inian. (Erevan, Armenia: Grakanut'ean ew arvesti t'angaran, 2003): 301-42.

——. "Verk' Hayastani (Haṛajaban)" [Preface to *Wounds of Armenia*] and "Mets azg erek' mateanov (urvagits)" [Great Nation with Just Three Books (An Outline)] in *Khach'atur Abovian: Verk' Hayastani, voghb hayrenasiri, patmakan vep*, ed. Gurgen Gasparian. (Erevan, Armenia: Grakanut'ean ew arvesti t'angaran, 2004).

PUBLISHED MEMOIRS

Gevorgian, Vardan. "Glukh-Glkhi Shēmsin het" [Tête-à-tête with Shēms]. *Armenia* [Buenos Aires] 12 November 1959.

Mkhit'arian, Gurgēn. "Hmayeak Shēms." *Hayrenik' Daily* [Boston] 3 May 1952: 1. Trans. by Vahé Baladouni and John Gery, "A Portrait of Hmayeak Shēms." *Ararat* [New York] Spring 1999.

Momchian, Perch. "Chashka chai" [Cup of Tea]. *Horizon* [Montreal] 30 March 1992: 9-12.

Shahpaz, Step'an. "Hmayeak Shēmsĕ zor chanch'ts'a" ["The Hmayeak Shēms I Knew"]. *Horizoni grakan havelvats* [Montreal] January 2002: 13-14.

UNPUBLISHED LETTERS AND MEMOIRS

All unpublished letters and memoirs are addressed to Vahé Baladouni.

Arshakuni, H. [Hovakim Hovakimian]. "The Talented Dervish: H. Shēms." Memoir. [c.1953.]
Fntk'ian, Ervand. Letter. 22 May 1952.
Fntk'ian, Ervand. Memoir. 24 February 1953.
Geghard, H. Letters. 2 May, 3 June, 7 August, 22 September 1953.
Gevorgian, Vardan. Letter. 16 November 1952.
Gevorgian, Vardan. Memoir. 11 June 1952.
Khach'aturian, Garegin Archbishop. Letters. 30 October and 4 December 1952.
Mkhit'arian, Gurgēn. Letter. 22 October 1952.
Parsamian, M. Letter. 3 June 1952.
Shahpaz, Step'an. Letters. 14 April 1952 and 8 February 1953.
TerVardanian, Gurgēn. Letter. 18 February 1953.
T'agvorian, Gabriel. Letters. 20 November 1952 and 10 November 1953.

REVIEWS

K'ristinian, Gēvorg. 1995. Review of *Ēntir Erker*, by Hmayeak Shēms. *Azparēz* [California] 4 April: 15.

Momchian, Perch. 1995. Review of *Ēntir Erker*, by Hmayeak Shēms. *Horizoni grakan havelvats* [Montreal] January: 9-11.

Oshakan, Vahē. 1995. Review of *Ēntir Erker,* by Hmayeak Shēms. *Haṛaj* [Haratch] [Paris] 15 March: 2.
Puchiganian, Atom. 2003. Review of *Hmayeak Shēmsi khosk'erun erazhshtagirk'ĕ* [Songbook on the Lyrics of Hmayeak Shēms] by Hmayeak Shēms. *Horizoni grakan havelvats* [Montreal] December.

GENERAL WORKS ON ARMENIAN HISTORY, LITERATURE, AND CULTURE

A reading list of scholarly yet accessible works on Armenian Geography, History, Church, Language, Literature, Art, Architecture, and Culture:

Abrahamian, Levon, and Nancy Sweezy, eds. *Armenian Folk Arts, Culture, and Identity.* Bloomington, IN: Indiana University Press, 2001.
"Armenia." *Dictionary of the Middle Ages.* 1983.
"Armenia." *New Grove Dictionary of Music and Musicians.* 2001.
Bardakjian, Kevork B., comp. *A Reference Guide to Modern Armenian Literature, 1500-1920.* Detroit, MI: Wayne State University Press, 2000.
Dadrian, Vahakn N. *The History of the Armenian Genocide: Ethnic Conflict from the Balkans to Anatolia to the Caucasus.* Providence, RI: Berghahn Books, 1995.
Der Nersessian, Sirarpie. *The Armenians.* New York: Praeger Publishers, 1970.
Hewsen, Robert H. *Armenia: A Historical Atlas.* Chicago: University of Chicago Press, 2001.
Hovannisian, Richard G., ed. *The Armenian People: from Ancient to Modern Times.* 2 Vols. New York: St Martin's Press, 1997.
Maksoudian, Krikor H. *Chosen of God: The Election of the Catholicos of all Armenians: from the Fourth Century to the Present.* New York: St Vartan Press, 1995.
Nersessian, Vrej. *The Bible in the Armenian Tradition.* London: The British Library, 2001.
———. *Treasures from the Ark: 1700 Years of Armenian Christian Art.* London: The British Library, 2001.
Novello, Adriano Alpago. *The Armenians: 2000 Years of Art and Architecture.* New York: Booking Press, 1995.
Thierry, Jean-Michel. *Armenian Art.* New York: Harry N. Abrams, 1989.
Thomson, R. W. *A Bibliography of Classical Armenian Literature to 1500 AD.* Brepols Turnhout: Corpvs Christianorvm, 1995. See also: *Supplement to "A Bibliography of Classical Armenian Literature to 1500 AD:" Publications 1993-2005, Le Muséon* 120, nos. 1-2 (2007): 163-223.

Index

Titles of Armenian works are given in their English translation. Numbers in *italics* refer to photographs.

Abdel Nasser, Colonel Gamal, 32
Abdul-Hamid II, 17
Abeghian, Manuk, 13
Abovian, Khach'atur, 52, 61, 81, 91n1
Acharian, Hrach'ya, 13
Aghayan, Ghazaros, 47
Aghbalian, Nikol, 33, 34, 35, 47, 89n35
Aharonian, Avetis, 8, 9
Akos (Beirut), 61
Alamein, El-, Egypt, 46
Alani, Hector, 27
Aleppo, Syria, 30
Alexandria, Egypt, 32, 45-46, 87n8, 87n9
Alishan Cultural Association, Alexandria, 45
Amirian, H., 33, 34
Anglo-Egyptian Treaty, 32
Anglo-Swiss Hospital, Alexandria, 63
Antoniades Café, Alexandria, 62
Ararat, Mount, 16
Aregents' H., 27, 43
Armenia: geography of, 15-16; history of, 16-17; Republic of (1918-1920), 3, 40; Republic of (1991-), 51; Wilsonian boundaries of, 40
Armenian Community of Alexandria, property owned by, 34
Armenian Community School, Constantsa, 21
Armenian Democratic Liberal Party, 34, 90n3 (Appendix B)
Armenian Genocide, news of, 17; *The Armenian Holocaust: A Bibliography Relating to the Deportations, Massacres, and Dispersion of the Armenian People*, 85n28; *The History of the Armenian Genocide*, 85n28
Armenian Girls' Home, Alexandria, 41
Armenian language, 15, 65, 88n25; fusion of Eastern and Western Armenian literary idioms, 65, 91n2
Armenian literature: gauging of, 52; nation's soul, clearest expression of, 51
Armenian Orphanage, Strunga, 21
Armenian Orphanage, Trabzon, 19
Armenian Progressive Party, 34

Armenian Revolutionary Federation, 34, 90n6, 90n3 (Appendix B)
Armenian SSR, 40
Arsharuni, Victoria, 41
Arvers, Félix, 61
assimilation, 57, 59
Astvatsaturian, A., 35
At'machian, Marie, 29, 87n2
attic apartment, Shēms's, 38, 40

Baladouni, Haykuhi, 18, 29-30, *39*, 41, 47
Baladouni, Surēn, 29-30, *39*
Baret, H., 27
Baudelaire, Charles, 61, 64
biography, critical, ix
Bolshevik Revolution, 18
Buddhism, 11-12
Burns, Robert, 83n3
Buzhank' (Paris), 36

cemeteries, 3
Ch'arents', Eghishē, 83n1 (Preface)

Darbinian, Mat'evos, 14
Dashnak Party. *See* Armenian Revolutionary Federation
death, news of Shēms's, 1
Deir el-Zor, Syria, 2
Denham, John, x
Durville, Henri, 36, 88n15

Ējmiatsin, Armenia, 12
The Emperor (Shant'), 46
Ēt'mēk'chian, Sahak, 7

Faruk, King, 32, 42
For One's Honor (Shirvanzadē), 46
Freud, Sigmund, 11
Frost, Robert, x
Fuad, King, 32, 42
funeral procession, Shēms's, 3
futurists, 47

Gautier, Théophile, 57, 61
Geghard, 65
Gēvorgian Academy, ējmiatsin, 12

Gēvorgian, Vardan, 21, 86n35
Gillet, Louis, 77, 91n4 (Appendix B)
grandmother, Shems's paternal, 5-6
Gregory of Narek, 52
Gümüşhané, Turkey, 4

Hairenik Monthly (Boston), 35
Hamazgayin Educational and Cultural Society, Alexandria, 45-46
Hay Dprots' (Cairo), 41
Haykaznian Gymnasium, Alexandria, 41, 49, 51
Hay Varzharan (Cairo), 35
Hnch'ak Party. *See* Social Democratic Hnch'akian Party
Hokhikian, Smbat, 63
Houssaper Daily (Cairo), 4
Houssaper Monthly (Cairo), 27
Hrazdan (Varna), 25

Ibrahimiya, Ramleh, 38
injustices, social, 7
insomnia, 61
Isahakian, Avetik', 8, 9, 42, 47

Kēonchian, Surēn, 63
Khach'atrian, A., 10
Khach'aturian, Garegin Vardapet, 19, 85n32
Khazhak, Garegin, 8, 9
Kipling, Rudyard, 18
Komitas Vardapet, 22, 86n36

Lemkin, Raphael, 17
Lusaworch'ian National School, Trabzon, 6

Mallarmé, Stéphane, 47
mariage forcé, Le (Molière), 46
Mediterranean Sea, 3
The Merchant of Venice (Shakespeare), 46
Merezhkovsky, Dmitry, 61
Mkhit'arian, Gurgēn, *50*, 90n1 (Appendix A)
Modern Egypt (Baring), 32
Mohammed Ali, 32
Momchian, Perch, 46

Muratbēkian, Khorēn (Katʻoghikos), 12-13, 85n23

nationalism, cultural, 60
nations, 35
Navasard (Bucharest), 25, 86n38
Near East Relief Agency, 21
Nietzsche, Friedrich, 10-11, 84n21
Nor Sharzhum (Cairo), 35
Nouzha Gardens. *See* Antoniades Café
Nupar Pasha, 32, 34

Oasis Coffeehouse, 47
Omar Khayyám, 45, 72
Oshakan, Hakob, 30, 49
Othello (Shakespeare), 46
Ottoman Empire, 5, 16, 17

Palayan School, Alexandria, 41
pan-Armenian mode of thought, Shēms's, 65
paradigm of the Armenian soul, Shēms's *œuvre*, 65
Paris, France, 36-37
Parnassians, 47
patriotism, 49, 60, 77
Pelouse, Rue, Ibrahimiya, 46
pen name, choice of, 26-27
Poghosian National School, Alexandria, 32, *33*, 34
political views, exchanging opposing, 77
The Princess of the Fallen Fortress (Shantʻ), 46
The Prophet (Gibran), 51
psychotherapy, Shēms practices, 40
Pushkin, Aleksandr, 57, 61

Ramkavar Party. *See* Armenian Democratic Liberal Party
Red Sultan. *See* Abdul-Hamid II
repatriation, 48-49
Rolland, Romain, 77, 91n4 (Appendix B)
Rommel, General Erwin, 45

Safavid Dynasty, 16
Sanasarian Academy, Karin, 7, 9

Sapʻrichʻian, Grigor, 5
Sapʻrichʻian, Tʻurvanta, 5
Sayat-Nova, 44-45, 52
Sēraytarian, Dr Mihran, 30
Sēraytarian, Paytsaṛ, 30, *39*
Shahpaz, Stepʻan, 90n2 (Appendix B)
Shantʻ, Levon, 35, 46, 47
Shaw, George Bernard, 11
Shelley, Percy Bysshe, x
Shēms, Hmayeak: "Abnormal Children in School" 35; "An Aborted Civilization" 43-44; "Alien" 58-59; "The Anvil" 54; "The Armenian Elite" 44; "Armenian Requiem" 61; "The Benefactor Snake" 6; "Burial" 2-3; "De Profundis" 55; "The Dervish" 12; "The Discontent of the Camels" 57; "The Education of the Will" 35; "Eternal Song" 18; "The Ghost of Tʻorgom" 59; "Great Nation with Just Three Books: An Outline" 52; "Homeward Bound!" 48; "Humanity and Its Crisis" 43; "Imagination and Moral Education" 41; "Kazel" 55; "La Donna" 54; "Let It Resound!" 44; "Let Us Respect the Children" 41; "The Man Who Found God" 6; "Metsaskʻanchʻ: Quo Vadis?" 85n26; "Monarch" 56; "My Nayiri" 53-54; "National Education" 35; "Night" 62; "Orphan" 23-24; "Our Times" 44; "Paths to the Summit" 57; "The Pig Victorious" 57; "Psychoanalysis" 35; "The School and Character" 35; "The School and the Home" 41; "Statue" 66-67; "That Sinful Woman" 36-37; "To the Poet" 26; "True Love" 54-55; "Why Did They Get Burned?" 85n25
Siruni, H. Ch., 25, 86n38
Social Democratic Hnchʻakian Party, 34
spiritualization, propensity toward, criterion of. *See* Armenian literature, gauging of
Srtadzor. *See* Sanasarian Academy
Srvandztiantsʻ, V., 35, 87n14
St Catherine, Place, 3

St Magdalene, Church of, 37
St Paul-St Peter Armenian Apostolic
    Church, Alexandria, 3
Surb P'rkich' Vank', Gümüşhanē, 4

T'agvorian, Gabriel, 33, 35, 89n35
T'ashian, Benyamin, 35, 91n4
    (Appendix C)
Tchahagir (Cairo), 29
Temirchian, Derenik, 47
Ter-Harut'iwnian, Barunak, 6, 7
Tērian, Vahan, 9, 11, 13
Ter-Mirak'ian, Hovhannes, 14
Tērtērian, Arsēn, 13
Ter-Vardanian, Gurgēn, 19
Thus Spake Zarathustra (Nietzsche), 10-11
tombstone, Shēms's, 3

Trabzon, Turkey, 5
translation, x
transliteration, xi
trauma, 22-24
T'umanian, Hovhannes, 47
Turkish atrocities. *See* Abdul-Hamid II;
    Armenian Genocide
Twilight Reveries (Tērian), 13
Tyutchev, Fyodor, 61

Valéry, Paul, 47
Varuzhan, Daniel, 11, 86n38
Verlaine, Paul, 36, 57, 61
Voskerich'ian, Fr Haykazun, 49

white massacre. *See* assimilation

Young Turk regime, 17

www.ingramcontent.com/pod-product-compliance
Lightning Source LLC
Chambersburg PA
CBHW030117010526
44116CB00005B/292